Everything I Know about Business and Marketing, I Learned from THE TOXIC AVENGER

● ● ●

Everything I Know about Business and Marketing, I Learned from THE TOXIC AVENGER

(One Man's Journey to Hell's Kitchen and Back)

JEFFREY W. SASS

Foreword by Lloyd Kaufman

ISBN-13: **9781544219240**
ISBN-10: **1544219245**
Library of Congress Control Number: 2017903574
CreateSpace Independent Publishing Platform
North Charleston, South Carolina

For my family: my parents, David and Evelyn; my sister, Diane; and my wonderful children, Zachary, Ethan, and Olivia, all of whom put up with me always and always knew I had a book in me somewhere. (They just never dreamed it would be in Tromaville.) Thanks for your constant love and support.

For Sue, who always encourages me to write and always encourages me.

For Lloyd, Michael, the Troma Team, and, of course, Toxie.

And for you. I am grateful you are here, and I hope the time you take to read my words proves enjoyable and worthwhile.

CONTENTS

FOREWORD

When I wrote my first book, the Tromatic tome *All I Need to Know about Filmmaking I Learned from The Toxic Avenger: The Shocking True Story of Troma Studios*, on page 210 I wrote that Jeff Sass was "probably the best Troma employee ever..." Well, of course, that couldn't possibly still be true. After all, when Jeff decided to leave Troma to pursue a real career, we replaced him with a kid named James Gunn. Now, James actually helped me write *All I Need to Know about Filmmaking*...and James has gone on to become one of the most talented and commercial directors living today (yeah, that *Guardians of the Galaxy* James Gunn), and he still talks to me. So, clearly, James Gunn was the best Troma employee ever.

That said, Sass was all right, even though he refused to sleep with me.

A fellow Ivy League graduate with an actual reputation and work experience when we hired him, Jeff Sass was the exception to our typical Troma Team employee, but we gave him a chance, and miraculously he not only survived but thrived during his seven-year stint on the dark side. He created the world-famous slogan "The First Super Hero from New Jersey." You'll read about that in chapter 4.

During Jeff's tenure, and with his inspiration and input, we experienced some of the golden years of Troma, becoming Troma Entertainment. Jeff was instrumental in turning Toxie, an R-Rated movie featuring a child getting his head squashed by the wheel of an automobile, into a delightful, highly rated, environmentally correct cartoon for kiddies on Fox TV Saturday morning. He also launched a huge licensing and merchandising division. We advanced into the computer age under Jeff's geek guidance and made some of our most ambitious, and now-classic, films with Jeff on the producing line, including *Troma's War* and *Sgt. Kabukiman, NYPD*. While Jeff's former stature in the film industry dwindled, Troma's star rose, and Troma's rose bloomed thanks in large part to Jeff Sass's many talents and contributions.

As for this book, while Jeff may no longer be Troma's best employee ever, he may have written the best book on Troma ever. And more important, he has managed to turn his experiences in Tromaville into a veritable MBA course for anyone interested in entrepreneurship, business, and marketing. Dear reader, you hold in your hand an extremely entertaining and funny look behind the scenes and under Kabukiman's kimono, but within Sass's Troma tales are real, very meaningful lessons of business value for everyone, including me! And 2017 marks my fiftieth year of making movies nobody sees.

Now, about that James Gunn guy...

Lloyd Kaufman
Cofounder, Troma

INTRODUCTION: LIGHTS, CAMERA, ACTION!

There are a lot of similarities between making movies and starting companies. Film producers and directors are as much entrepreneurs as anyone who might create or aspire to create a Silicon Valley start-up. The purpose of this book is to draw valuable lessons in business and marketing from my experiences making movies—not in Hollywood, mind you, but rather in Tromaville. Since my filmmaking days, I've been a start-up cofounder, COO, CEO, and currently a CMO, and I don't think I ever could have survived the C-suite if I hadn't had the experience of making B-movies.

• • •

Early in my career, I spent seven and a half years working for Troma, the low-budget film studio probably best known for the cult-classic action/horror film *The Toxic Avenger*. As I am sure you *must* know, *The Toxic Avenger* is the heartwarming story of Melvin Junko, a lowly mop boy who, teased and taunted, falls into a vat of radioactive waste and emerges as...the Toxic Avenger—the First Superhero from New Jersey!

As a movie, *The Toxic Avenger* was sloppy, gory, cheesy, tasteless, and perhaps even unsavory. But as a character, the Toxic Avenger (now affectionately known as "Toxie") was remarkably endearing, especially for a hideously deformed creature of superhuman size and strength. In his 1986 review of the film, Stephen Holden of the *New York Times* said *The Toxic Avenger* "may be trash, but it has a maniacally farcical sense of humor, and Tromaville's evildoers are dispatched in ingenious ways."

The oft-warped brainchild of two Yale graduates, Lloyd Kaufman and Michael Herz, Troma has indeed been ingenious in creating a world outside the Hollywood norm, their own Tromaville, where the filmmakers are beholden to no force other than their own off-kilter creative muse. The proof of their ingenuity? Today Troma Entertainment still lives on, over forty years old and arguably the world's oldest independent film studio. That monstrous creature Toxie? He's gone on to survive three sequels and a Saturday-morning cartoon spin-off, along with the requisite comic books, toys, games, and apparel. A rumored "big studio" remake even threatened to star Arnold Schwarzenegger as Toxie.

The Troma Team is notorious for giving young, inexperienced aspiring filmmakers a chance to work, often way over their heads and always way under their expected minimum wage. But the experience, as they say, is priceless. It was for me. And as I hope this book will expose, my lessons from Tromaville extended far beyond my celluloid dreams. While many former Tromites went on to impressive (and more traditional) Hollywood careers (including the likes of actor Kevin Costner and director James Gunn), my own post-Tromatic career led me down the path of a marketer and tech entrepreneur. I think I am pretty good at what I do. I've had many great experiences in the business world since I emigrated from Tromaville in 1994. But if I am truly honest with myself, I must admit that I couldn't have done it without Toxie.

Making movies is hard work, especially making movies on a shoestring budget. Actually, we couldn't even afford shoe strings—we had Velcro budgets! But I learned a lot: how to mix theatrical blood, how to make a ripe cantaloupe substitute for a head being crushed...but making movies also taught me a lot about business and entrepreneurship.

In truth, a film production is like a start-up on steroids. You go from screenplay (business plan) to product completion in a matter of months. You have to hire, fire, build up, tear down, raise money, spend money, rally the troops, fight deadlines and external forces, and make constant compromises, all the while fighting to stay the course and make the best film (i.e., product) you can. Teamwork and camaraderie, on and off the set, make a big difference (culture), and in the end, success or failure comes from ultimately finding an audience (satisfied customers).

Nobody sets out to make a bad film, just like nobody starts a company with the intention of failing.

Chapter 1

● ● ●

WELCOME TO TROMAVILLE

New York, just like I pictured it. Actually, it was New York, just as I always knew it, having grown up in Forest Hills, Queens, and acclimated at a young age to the Q60 bus to Manhattan and the E, F, G, N, and RR subway lines into "the City." Tromaville, on the other hand, was less familiar.

I was working for a relatively unknown TV-and-film-distribution company, Satori Entertainment, my first job out of college, when I first heard about "the Troma Guys." Satori, an interesting story in and of itself, was run by the late Ernie Sauer, in many ways a TV pioneer and visionary, who, among other things, started the first satellite-distributed radio service long before the likes of Sirius and XM Radio were a twinkle in their founders' eyes.

During my tenure at Satori, in the early '80s, the company achieved some notoriety as a leading importer of "English-language foreign films"— in other words, films from Australia, New Zealand, and Great Britain. We would obtain the North American rights to these films and license them to the burgeoning pay-TV market, including the early days of HBO and Showtime, and a small network of over-the-air STV (Subscription Television) services that were cropping up in a handful of markets around the country—all precursors to the cable-TV and home-video explosions that were on the cusp of arriving. We had a few early successes, like *Dot and the Kangaroo*, an Australian live-action and animated children's film, and Bruce Beresford's *Don's Party* as well as the early Mel Gibson film *Tim*, with Mel and Piper Laurie. In a few cases, we dabbled in releasing some of our imports in theaters, and for a while, we played host to an Australian Film Festival at the old D. W. Griffith Theater on East Fifty-Ninth Street.

Then the home-video revolution arrived, and our growing catalog of films found new value on VHS. *Dot and the Kangaroo* was licensed to Andre Blay's Magnetic Home Video, which eventually became Fox Home Video, and a new, lucrative market emerged. Along the way, we went public, and after Satori's IPO, we realized that it made sense to acquire more films and grow our library as our distribution channels into the developing pay-TV and home-video markets continued to expand and thrive. It was with such acquisitions in mind that I decided to call on "the Troma Guys," who, after all, were situated in "the Troma Building," a mere seven blocks north on Ninth Avenue from Satori headquarters, adjacent to the Port Authority Bus Terminal.

I had heard of Troma and the story of Lloyd and Michael's little film fiefdom. I may even have seen a Troma film or two. But mostly I was aware they had built a nice-sized library of low-budget films they had produced themselves or acquired from others: films I presumed would potentially have value in the growing pay-TV and syndicated-TV marketplace we were supplying. I gave them a call and was invited to come visit them.

Chapter 2

● ● ●

THE TROMA BUILDING

In the heart of Hell's Kitchen. Ninth Avenue and Forty-Ninth Street to be precise. A four-story walk-up brownstone that Lloyd and Michael had wisely purchased with the profits from one of their early hits, most likely the light T-and-A comedies *Waitress* and *Squeeze Play*. The north side of the brick-faced Troma Building was exposed, unadulterated, and clearly visible to all traffic heading downtown on Ninth Avenue. It was adorned with a giant-sized version of the one-sheet (movie parlance for a poster) of *The Toxic Avenger* movie and the greeting, "Welcome to Tromaville." Yes, as countless buses, cars, and taxis voyaged down Ninth Avenue into the famous Hell's Kitchen neighborhood, they were greeted not by graffiti but by the infamous hideously deformed creature of superhuman size and strength. A truly supersized Toxie, complete with a mop the size of a schoolyard flagpole. Heading south on Ninth Avenue, there was no question you had arrived in Tromaville.

That small investment in Manhattan real estate was one of the many business and marketing strokes of genius executed by Lloyd and Michael and it, quite literally, put Troma on the map (at least on the map of the West Side of New York City). Think about it: Which other independent film studio could afford billboard advertising in midtown Manhattan, albeit the somewhat seedier side of said midtown? Still, it was great exposure, and it was free.

Speaking of free, the ground floor of the Troma Building had a retail space that was rented out to a variety of tenants over the years. The building was bought for cash and had no mortgage, so as long as the rent from the retail tenant covered the cost of insurance and real-estate taxes, Troma's film business could occupy the rest of the building essentially rent-free. This low overhead advantage probably kept the company alive during the many lean times. And there were many lean times.

Chapter 3

● ● ●

MEET THE MOGULS

There were three stories above the street-level storefront and countless stories within those three stories. On the first floor (actually the second floor of the building, but the first floor of the Troma offices), after climbing the narrow stairs, one entered the main office landing. To use the word "reception" area would be disingenuous, as visitors were not received as much as they were ignored, and once noticed, most likely put to work.

Two uncomfortable and mismatched office chairs were against the wall to your left. Before you was a beat-up desk, most likely occupied by a heavily tattooed and pierced young person of indiscriminate gender who had been "working" for Troma anywhere from two hours to two days. If they had survived for longer than two days, they would no longer be assigned to the front desk but would probably have been reassigned to head up theatrical sales, or edit trailers on one of the flatbeds on the fourth floor, or given some other critically important task they were grossly ill prepared and underqualified for.

Eventually, some screaming and yelling would emanate from behind the smoke-glass walls of the office diagonally opposite the "reception" desk. The yelling was often followed by the slamming of phone receivers (the old, heavy plastic kind, with cords and such) and perhaps the sound of books, magazines, and film cans being tossed across the room and into the walls. If you were lucky, the screaming and yelling would get the attention of the heavily tattooed and pierced young person of indiscriminate gender who would finally notice your presence. "Oh," he/she/it would say. "May I help you?"

"I am here to see Lloyd and Michael."

And before he/she/it could respond further, Lloyd himself would come bursting out of the office, screaming like a banshee, "What is it? Asshole time?" Blasting past you as if you were the invisible man himself, Lloyd would light into the reception person as a lion attacks its prey, tearing them apart, psychological limb by psychological limb, until they either quit, broke down in tears, or simply accepted their fate and moved on to the next outrageous task Lloyd would assign to them.

And then his attention would drift to his unannounced guest, and zap! Kaufman transforms into the charming, almost delightful, intelligent, and affable Yale graduate (albeit a slightly scruffy one) you may have imagined.

"Come in, come in."

Their office was a cluttered and messy room, large enough for two desks facing each other, with a sizable chasm between, Michael to the left and Lloyd to the right. Set up for an intentional daily literal face-off, staring at each other with no privacy. By design, they could overhear each other's every phone call, and chime in from across the room. By design, they could argue over the smallest minutiae and yell and scream at each other with freedom and abandon whenever their muse manifest itself. It was manufactured mayhem. And, for them, it worked.

I sat in the aisle between them, shifting back and forth to face the speaker of the moment. It was funny. It was fun. We sort of all got along. I explained about Satori and asked about their video and TV syndication plans. They ignored me and asked if I'd like the tour of the Troma Building. Of course, I would. And up the stairs we went, starting at the top—the editing rooms.

The fourth floor of the Troma Building was arguably where the magic happened.

Chapter 4

● ● ●

TRAILER TRASH

aving huffed and puffed my way up to the fourth floor, I entered the editing lair. Here, there were a few seemingly ancient Moviola "flat-bed" film editing consoles. Remember, this was more or less predigital, and still in the age of film. Editing involved literally cutting and splicing strips of film and magnetic sound tapes in an attempt to make something cohesive. A film editor works with prints of the raw footage that was shot during production. When the edited film is finalized and approved by the director, it gets sent to a "negative cutter"—someone skilled in the art of carefully and cleanly handling the camera negatives. The negative cutter conforms the original film negative to the approved edit, and that cut negative, when married to optical effects and a fully mixed soundtrack, becomes the master from which all the prints are made, that eventually end up in theaters. This was 1985. The first nonlinear video editing systems were just being demonstrated and were several years away from being put to any practical use by filmmakers. And, anyway, Troma was decidedly "old school" in those days.

As I took my tour with Lloyd, he showed me a work in progress, a new trailer for the intentionally gross, soon to become legendary, Troma epic, *The Toxic Avenger*. The film had enjoyed some early notoriety but had yet to find its niche in B-movie history as the so-called cult classic it remains today. I don't think I had actually seen *The Toxic Avenger* at the time, but its reputation preceded it and I had a pretty good inkling as to what it was all about. My impression, from reviews and word of mouth, was that it was fairly gross and somewhat sophomoric, yet somehow charming and disarming because of an underlying sweetness and humor. Lloyd showed me the trailer in progress, which was fairly graphic and straightforward, and ended with a particularly dry and emotionless tag line, "A Different Kind of Hero!"

Lloyd asked me what I thought. I answered honestly. "Meh." My understanding was that part of the movie's appeal was that it had an element of comedy to it, despite the graphic, arguably tasteless violence. I felt the trailer, in the end, fell flat, largely because the tagline, "A Different Kind of Hero," didn't really convey *how* Toxie (or the movie for that matter) was indeed different. It was boring. It was plain.

"Well," said Lloyd, "What tagline would you use instead?"

I thought about it a moment and asked a question. I had done my homework and read up on the film. I knew that much of it was filmed across the Hudson River from Manhattan and that the locale had been worked into the story as Toxic's home. Like any good New Yorker, I also knew the various slurs and aspersions we'd lovingly cast at our Garden State neighbor. So, thinking fast I responded, "The Toxic Avenger is from Jersey City, right?"

"Uh, yeah," said Lloyd.

"So," I continued. "I'd use the tagline 'The First Superhero…from New Jersey!'—something that is an immediate wink to the audience, letting them know that there's a hint of comedy here too."

Lloyd paused a moment in deep thought. Then he repeated my suggestion aloud, quietly, like a freshly assigned mantra. "The First Superhero from New Jersey…That's great. Can we use it?"

"Sure," I said.

The trailer was changed. The posters too. And like that Toxie became the first superhero from New Jersey.

And that was the first of the many things I would end up writing for Troma.

The poster for *The Toxic Avenger* with the new, improved tagline

The lesson here, of course, and one I have used again and again since is to **share your ideas**. Don't be afraid to give someone a good idea or help them without expecting anything from it. Holding back your ideas because they are precious or valuable or because you are afraid someone will steal them, is just a way to hold yourself back. This is especially true when you are trying to get a job or a new client. Give them a tangible taste of what you are really capable of. Give them a sampling of your valuable ideas that they can use and benefit from whether they hire you or not. More often than not, if your ideas are good, you will get hired or get the client. If you allow your best ideas to be turned into secrets, you may never get to see your ideas put to use.

There's also a great lesson here from Lloyd's behavior. He listened! Even though it was probably he who came up with the original tagline, "A Different Kind of Hero," Lloyd was open to change and to new ideas, regardless of where they came from. Who was this Sass guy, anyway? He had just met me for the first time. I had no track record to speak of, and yet when Lloyd heard a good idea, a better choice, he was ready and willing to discard what he had already done and make a change that he perceived to be for the better. And it cost money to change the trailer and the posters and flyers. But it was the right move.

How open are you to accepting suggestions and new ideas?

Chapter 5

● ● ●

WORKING FREE-LANCE

loyd, Michael, and I hit it off quite well, and I was immediately fond of them and enamored by the crazy, self-contained, and self-controlled world they had created for themselves in that messy building on Ninth Avenue. But despite our good connection, they had absolutely zero interest in doing any business with Satori. Troma was, and is, fiercely independent, and if anyone were going to distribute their movies to pay TV and beyond, it would be them (or someone willing to pay an exorbitant fee in the form of an offer they could not refuse.) So we parted ways as friends.

Until, some six months later, when I decided to leave my job at Satori to become a screenwriter.

I had been with Satori for five and a half years and at that point felt I had gone as far as I could within the organization in its current structure. It had been a great run for me, and I had gained incredible experiences there, producing the early Cable TV show, *Celebrity* with hostess Alison Steele, traveling the world to film festivals, and much, much more. But my personal creative itch was screaming to be scratched. I wanted to be a screenwriter and make movies. While Satori gave me many opportunities to be creative, it was clear the company was on a path focused more on distribution than production, and I wanted to make stuff.

So I struck out on my own, with the initial goal of writing (and hopefully selling) original screenplays. I got to work on my very first screenplay,

Wunderkind, and upon completion, I sent it over to Lloyd and asked him to read it. While a comedy, *Wunderkind* wasn't a Troma-style film, but I was hoping to get feedback from someone who actually made movies.

Lloyd was kind enough to read my script, and he and Michael invited me to visit them again in Tromaville to see what I was up to. I once again found myself sitting in the kooky chasm between the desks of Messrs. Kaufman and Herz. I was young and green and passionately told them how "I wanted to write and make movies." They said that based on *Wunderkind* they thought I could write and if I wanted to, I could write a screenplay for them. They had an idea for a story.

They offered to pay a little something if I was able to turn their story idea into a full screenplay. My recollection was that it was around $1,200, payable when an acceptable script was delivered. I probably would have done it for free, but it was even more exciting to have a "paid" writing assignment. I was briefed on their story idea, took notes and their treatment, and got to work on it.

During the eighteen months after leaving Satori, I wrote three full screenplays (*Wunderkind*, *Deep Cover*, and the *Troma Project*). I also formed a production company with Academy Award–winning animator Jimmy Picker and another partner to write and produce a clay-animated and live-action special, *My Friend Liberty*, which aired on CBS in the summer of 1986 to mark the hundredth anniversary of the Statue of Liberty. Troma paid me my small fee, I made a modest fee from *My Friend Liberty*, and one of my screenplays, *Deep Cover*, was optioned by a Hollywood producer. I also got married, and we eventually became pregnant.

I thought *My Friend Liberty* would immediately lead to tons of work for our burgeoning production company and that I was on my way. But I was way off in my naive enthusiasm. More production work was not forthcoming, and the dwindling funds and insecurities of the freelance life were not conducive to starting a family, not to mention supporting one. I needed a job. A real job. I settled for working for Troma.

Chapter 6

● ● ●

BECOMING A FULL-TIME TROMITE

Back at the Troma Building, I told Lloyd and Michael that I was ready for full-time employment. I wanted to make movies. They thought that was nice. But, they weren't in production on anything at the moment, and besides, they didn't really pay much to the folks they hired for production work since there were so many willing and eager to work for literal peanuts (and a cold beverage to wash the nuts down with) just to gain some hands-on experience on a real film crew. If I wanted a working wage, I'd need to do something more important than making the movies, I'd have to sell them.

Given my background in acquisitions and distribution over at Satori, they thought I'd be the perfect guy to start moving Troma into the blooming home-video and pay-TV markets. It wasn't much of a salary, but it was a real job. It wasn't what I wanted to do, but it was a step closer to making movies, and I figured (correctly, as it turned out) that once they were actually in production again, I'd find a way to get more intimately involved in that process, along with my sales responsibilities.

We came to an agreement and shook hands. And Lloyd walked me out into the main office, swiped a mess of papers off the corner of a desk where there was a phone, and pulled up an orphaned chair. "Here you go, Sass," as he pointed to the workspace he just created. "Welcome to Tromaville!"

And so it began.

Chapter 7

● ● ●

BRANDING BEGINS ON THE GROUND FLOOR

Greetings from Tromaville! That was how every single bit of correspondence began—from the letters we'd type on typewriters and word processors in the early days, to the telexes, faxes, and eventually e-mails we would send. The lessons I learned about building a brand and brand consistency while a member of the Troma Team have stuck with me for more than twenty years. What was this offbeat, off-kilter, often tasteless runt of a movie studio doing that was so compelling from the standpoint of branding? First of all, they were building a *brand*, something in those days arguably no film company except Disney had done.

Nobody went to see a movie because it was a "Paramount Picture" or because it was from "Warner Brothers." They went to see a movie because it starred Robert De Niro or Meryl Streep, or because it was based on a favorite book, or was directed by Martin Scorsese or Francis Ford Coppola or another star director. The studio was secondary and largely meaningless to the moviegoer. Except for Disney. People, especially families, went to see a movie because it was a Disney movie. And Troma. Our fans would go see (and still go see) a movie because it was a Troma movie. Whether it is *Redneck Zombies* or *Tromeo and Juliet* or some other odd title they never heard of; as long as it was Troma, our fans would show up. Why? Because, like Disney, based on the brand, they knew what to expect. That's what branding is all about—*establishing trusted consumer expectations.* It doesn't matter if the expectations are for family-friendly fare or tasteless, sophomoric gore, as long as the brand message is well established and consistent, it works.

And a strong brand has to be rooted in something accessible. Something consumers can relate to either by association or by aspiration. Something that makes them feel that by supporting the brand, they are part of a community or tribe of like-minded consumers and fans. This is as true for toothpaste as it is for a cookie or, in this book's case, a low-budget, independent movie studio.

Troma has achieved remarkable brand affinity over forty years and around the globe by creating an inclusive universe—Tromaville, where everyone is part of the "Troma Team." This concept is hammered into every Troma employee and everyone who watches a Troma movie. From the opening logo to every Troma film, the message is clear. This is "a Troma Team release." There is no "i" in Team, and there is definitely no "I" in Tromaville. Well, I suppose there actually is the letter "i" in the word "Tromaville," but aside from that grammatical digression, once you enter the land of Tromaville, you must always put the Troma Team first, literally and figuratively.

Chapter 8

● ● ●

THE POWER OF WE

Wheee! Rather, "we." If Troma were to publish their own *Elements of Troma Style*, two things would happen. First, William Strunk Jr. would roll over in his grave. Second, the book would begin with the statement, "Never, ever, ever, say 'I' when speaking or writing on behalf of the Troma Team. It is *always* 'we.' There is no 'I.'"

This simple rule was enforced by Lloyd as if it were gospel. More than gospel, as if it were the single most important thing above all other important things. As if by violating this one seemingly simple rule, one would be engaging in the most heinous act of corporate malfeasance. In Tromaville saying, "I" was a crime. You as an individual did not exist. Only the Troma Team existed. You did not do anything. Whatever you think you may have done, you didn't do it. We did. We, we, whee!

If Lloyd caught wind of a letter going out with "I this" or "I that" in it, he would go ballistic. It didn't matter who you were or what the topic or contents of the correspondence was; you had to use "we" instead of "I." Always. Without exception. And that went for Lloyd's own correspondence as well. In Tromaville, though seemingly a royal pain in the ass, the use of the Royal "we" reigned supreme.

And it was great. And it was a great lesson, not only in building a brand but also in creating a culture. Think about it. By enforcing this one simple rule, the notion of being a part of a team was deeply instilled in every employee at every level. From unpaid students and interns to barely paid senior executives, we were all collectively the Troma Team. Everything we did was to support the Troma Team.

As important was the subtle message this consistent use of "we" instilled in the outside world, even if they didn't quite realize it. Something was different and special about Troma, and you could sense it from every letter or e-mail that always started with "Greetings from Tromaville" and never put self ahead of team. And once you got used to it, it felt better to say "we" than "I." We were a team and saying "I" felt like you were taking something away from the group. On the other hand, after a while, saying "we" made you feel good. It reassured you that you were indeed part of a tribe (albeit an odd and sometimes creepy one).

To this day, I prefer to say "we" in business correspondence, and it took me a long time after my tenure in Tromaville to not feel a touch of guilt when I wrote "I" in a business letter or e-mail. In truth, "we" is often much better and more accurate. Just like making a movie, business is a very collaborative process. Unless you are truly a sole proprietor, it is unlikely that there are many, if any, business projects or accomplishments that are truly achieved by you alone. If you are an employee or an employer, you are part of a team, and for most things you might take credit for, just saying "I" is a bit disingenuous. And even if you had the lead or did most of the work yourself, saying "we" lets you share the love, and sets a great leadership example. Even today, I often find myself cringing in meetings when I hear someone spouting "I did this" and "I did that" when I know, as does everyone else in the room know, that the person shining the light on him- or herself had lots of help from other members of the organization.

Here's an exercise: Go forty-eight hours deliberately using "we" instead of "I," and see what happens. How does it make you feel? How do your coworkers and others treat you when you credit "we" for everything?

Chapter 9

● ● ●

OLD YELLER (AND BE YOUR BRAND)

The most valuable trait to understand and recognize in someone or something is consistency. We, humans, are hardwired for pattern recognition. We are built to spot things that are consistent, for a pattern is simply something that appears or occurs consistently. We can deal with patterns. We can deal with consistency. When I first arrived in Tromaville, I quickly learned that Lloyd and Michael were yellers and screamers. Especially during film production.

Author's note: We realize that the previous chapter espoused the importance of using "we" instead of "I," and yet here we are using "I" throughout this book. We are distraught over this blatant contradiction and recognize that we may lose some credibility and perhaps even some of your trust. We feel truly awful about this and hope we have not let you down. However, in the context of a somewhat autobiographical tale (after all, the subtitle of this Tromatic tome is "one man's journey to Hell's Kitchen and back"), the author felt we could take creative license—and risk it being revoked—and share the stories and lessons herein from the author's unique, first-person perspective. We hope you will forgive us. And now we return you to chapter 9, already in progress.

When the pressure was on, the yelling and screaming was also on. And on at a very loud volume. Before joining the Troma Team, I don't think

I really understood what it meant to be yelled at. Sure, as a child I had done stupid stuff to the point of provoking one or both of my parents to raise their voice at me. But never in business had I been the object of such verbal aggression. At first, it was shocking and upsetting to me, and since it was such a foreign experience, I took it personally and assumed that I was being yelled at for something I had done.

But soon the patterns revealed themselves, and as a genetically sound human, I came to recognize that the yelling had absolutely nothing to do with me. It was simply the way the mad moguls operated. They were screamers. They were yellers. And they screamed and yelled consistently, at anyone and everyone. They screamed and yelled at each other. Hell, they set up an office environment where they faced each other all day, probably (consciously or not) to facilitate easy yelling.

And once my pattern recognition light bulb went off, the yelling no longer bothered me. Consistency is easy to deal with because your expectations are set and accurate. If someone always yells, you always know what to expect. If someone is consistently an asshole, you know what to expect. You understand their pattern and can deal with them accordingly and with less stress. It is the inconsistent people who challenge us. The person who rarely yells and then suddenly, unexpectedly screams, will truly throw us off. The person modeled on Jekyll and Hyde, who is sometimes your best friend and sometimes a maniacal asshat, and you never know which to expect, that is the most difficult person to deal with. They are unpredictable. They don't fit a pattern.

So, the yellers were easy.

And to their credit, by the time I left Tromaville they had calmed down quite a bit, and the old yelling, with true vim and vigor, was seldom experienced.

So, what does all this talk of yelling have to do with branding? Consistency. It is all about consistency.

An effective brand must always stand for the same thing. An effective brand must be consistent. What your brand is consistent about perhaps matters far less than the fact that you are consistent in presenting the brand values. Know your brand. Decide what it stands for, good or bad, and get behind it consistently. The more consistent your brand message is, the more lasting it will be. Look at the great brands. If you ask ten people what those brands stand for, you will get ten very similar answers. They all have the same expectations of the brand.

At Troma, the brand image was one that resonated deeply with our fans. We were a team, The Troma Team, and if you were a fan, you were a part of that team. You were welcome in Tromaville. We took our business seriously, but we didn't take ourselves too seriously. If they had not already been violently ripped from our throats, our collective Troma tongues were held firmly in cheek.

Understanding and appreciating the Troma brand was critical to my success in Tromaville.

Chapter 10

● ● ●

FIND SOMETHING TO BELIEVE IN

The common thread you will hear people say is that you should "pursue your passion" and find a job you are passionate about. The truth is, in my humble opinion, often the opposite. Most people do not find a job or career that exactly matches their deep inner passion. But that doesn't mean that being passionate about what you do is not important. It is. But you may need to work a bit to find that passion.

If I am honest, despite the fact I worked for Troma for more than seven years and was intimately involved in the writing, producing, marketing, and sales of many of their signature films, I was never actually a hardcore fan of Troma movies. As a moviegoer, I tolerated them. As a creative, I got caught up in the muse of the moment and immersed myself in every production wholeheartedly. I was able to do this for two reasons.

One: I loved the act of making movies. The creative collaboration was infectious. The concentrated energy and intense focus on one common task was exhilarating. Making a movie, especially an independent film, where the lines of responsibility are perhaps more blurred than in a more formal production, is like going to summer camp (and is for around the same amount of time). For roughly eight weeks, you are practically living with a bunch of strangers with a common interest. Together you are in your own little world for this intense, but short, time period, more or less cut off from or at least not focused on, the rest of the world.

I loved summer camp. I loved making movies too.

The second reason I was a great citizen of Tromaville was that I came to truly appreciate our fans. While maybe these films were not necessarily my cup of tea, I could recognize that there were a lot of loyal tea drinkers out there who really, really loved and enjoyed what we were brewing. Troma fans are loyal and dedicated. They are free spirits, free thinkers (and, if they transitioned from fan to employee, mostly free workers). Regardless, their love and appreciation for our movies was, and is, real. The joy and satisfaction I saw in our fans made me proud to be in a position to help bring our films to them. The work we were doing, as campy and sometimes childish as it was, was anticipated and more importantly, appreciated by our fans.

So, I worked for our fans. I made silly movies I didn't necessarily want to watch myself because I knew there were people out there who did want to watch. I became passionate about our films because I knew our fans were. My passion was real, and it fueled all the hard work I did to keep the Troma dream alive. I could get inside the heads of our fans, and from their perspective, I could see, enjoy, and contribute to the awesomeness that was, and is, Troma.

There's a great lesson in this for anyone in business. There are going to be times in your career where you are doing something that is not so great, or that you are not particularly fond of. You still need to do it well, and to do it well you need to embrace it. You need to find something about it that you can love. Find some element of the work that you can be honestly and deeply passionate about. There is always something.

I found the fans. I didn't have to be passionate about the movies themselves as I was passionate about delivering to the fans exactly what they wanted. I wanted to make great Troma movies—the best we could—to satisfy those fans, and I came to love doing so.

It's like any good relationship. Eventually, you come to love the whole package, even if, in the beginning, it was just certain bits of him or her that you were attracted to.

Find something to believe in. It is the only way to succeed.

Chapter 11

● ● ●

SHOW UP!

Question: What do you think is the most important thing when it comes to making a movie? A good script? A talented director? A great DP? (Director of Photography).

Answer: None of the above.

The bottom line is, every day of production you need three things to be able to make a movie, and without these three things, well, basically then you are fucked. Without fail you need the following:

1. A working camera
2. Film (or in this day and age, ample digital storage to record on)
3. Actors and actresses to perform in front of the camera

Without those three things, it doesn't matter how good the script is or how talented the director is. It doesn't matter if the DP has won awards, or if the lighting is perfect or if the location is amazing. No camera, no movie. No film, no movie. No performers, no movie. Those are the basics. You must show up every single day with those three things as the bare minimum. But they are more than the bare minimum. They are the bare essentials. Or, as they'd say in *Jungle Book*, "the bear necessities."

When I worked on my first Troma movie, the epic masterpiece, *Troma's War*, I learned these lessons. I was the associate producer, and one of my first assignments was to "protect the cameras" and make sure all the principal actors and actresses showed up on time. Protect the cameras? WTF? It turned out, once before, while filming an earlier cinematic epic, a rogue group of angry Teamsters stole the Troma camera truck overnight, literally bringing that production to a costly halt.

You see, as a (very) low-budget operation, Troma makes nonunion, independent films and back in the late '80s, especially when shooting in New York, the powerful Teamsters Union didn't like that. Even though we always played by the rules and had permits and permissions, often with the kind support of the New York City Mayor's or New York State Governor's Film Commissions, the Teamsters would go out of their way to attempt to make our lives miserable and disrupt our production.

Perhaps it was because it was before the dawn of the World Wide Web and free Internet porn, and those lonely Teamster souls had nothing better to do with their time than leave their homes and families on a weekend to come harass the Troma Team. Perhaps that was it, and now with the Web readily available via the mobile device in their sweaty palms, perhaps now they don't bother the Indy filmmakers as much. Perhaps.

But back then they were nasty, and I was warned. Protect the camera truck. That was *my* responsibility. The camera truck was a rented U-Haul truck that was custom decked out by our team to house all the rented camera and lighting equipment for the shoot. We may have been low budget, but our largest expense, and thus the most-prized asset, was all the professional (and valuable) 35-mm camera and lighting equipment we rented from the same well-known NYC rental houses that served the "Hollywood" crews when they were in town. Fully loaded with all our essential gear, the camera truck was the first vehicle to arrive on the set every day, and the last vehicle to leave each night after it was carefully packed, every lens, film can, and camera body in its designated, custom-fit place. Where to park the camera truck each night was a critical decision, because, once before, those tricky Teamsters had stolen our truck, rented cameras and all, right out of a locked and guarded NYC parking lot.

I had to protect the camera truck. It was not going to get stolen or disabled on my watch. Fortunately, we filmed most of *Troma's War* in

Peekskill, NY and at the National Guard training facility, Camp Smith. At the time, I was living in Rockland County, about a twenty-five-minute ride away, through the winding roads of Bear Mountain State Park. So, I would have the camera truck park behind my house every night, hidden from view from the main road. With the fear of Teamsters deeply ingrained in my younger, impressionable mind, I remember the first few nights, waking up at the simplest sound to look out the window and make sure the truck and its precious contents were still there, behind my humble abode.

The basics. Protect the camera (and the film, which was also stored in the truck). Make sure it showed up on set, first thing, every single day. And don't forget the actors and actresses.

There's a reason the transportation captain is one of the most important people on a movie crew, and more importantly a reason that captain makes certain that a car and driver was waiting outside the apartment or home of every principal actor before they even were awake, ready to herd those sleepy thespians to the day's location long before they were actually needed. Despite our low-budget operation, even our talent got picked up by a car and driver every day (granted, on a Troma set it was usually a wide-eyed intern in their own beat-up vehicle, but it was a car and driver nonetheless). We did this not because we wanted to treat them special or like a "star" (although many of them took it that way), but rather because of the basics—no actors, no movie.

Understanding the necessity of the basics was a good lesson. In business, it is very easy to get caught up in the detritus, in the details of the moment, and lose sight of the simple things that are actually far more important.

Exercise: What are your basics, your "bear" necessities? What are the three things you should be doing every day to ensure that you are keeping your business or marketing on track? What are your equivalents of the camera, film, and actors?

Chapter 12

● ● ●

SINK OR SWIM

The only source of knowledge is experience.

—ALBERT EINSTEIN

And thus, Tromaville has perhaps been the greatest film school ever. Literally, no application process or qualifications required. No tuition. Virtually every student is a scholarship case. Show up eager and ready, and you are likely to be put to work. Present even a modicum of initiative, and you are likely to be given a chance to operate at a level you have no reasonable qualifications for, and in 90 percent of the time, no chance of actually being any good at it or succeeding. More than likely you'll quit, sobbing and broken, and never set foot on a movie set again, let alone say anything remotely kind about your personal experience in Tromaville.

But, if you're in that 10 percent who make it, who actually rise to the occasion, set the bullshit aside, and get the job done, your stint in Tromaville will be the best experience you could ever have, and you will learn career-inspiring and career-changing lessons. It's film school on steroids. It's sink or swim.

Never underestimate the power of just doing it. There's a reason the famed Nike slogan has endured all these years. "Just do it" is often the best way to grow and learn (and it sounds a hell of a lot better than "sink or swim"). But, in Tromaville, where madness and opportunity abound, anyone at any time may be given the opportunity to step up to walk the plank, dive into the unknown, and truly sink or swim. Never directed a second unit? Now's your chance. Never designed and sewn a wardrobe from scratch? Now's your chance. Never written lines of dialogue at 1:00 a.m. that actors would speak in front of the camera at 7:00 a.m.? Now's your chance. Ever convince the monsignor of a local church to allow you to shoot scenes of violence, drug use, and debauchery inside their lovely chapel? I did (and I had no idea what I was doing...the first time).

Experienced talent costs money. Giving experience to newbies costs nothing. It's hit or miss, sink or swim. Most will implode and fuck up, but many will do just fine, and some will be amazing, and somehow, everything will get done, and the film will get made.

That's Troma. Better to be finished than to be perfect.

That's a lesson, too. The best way to learn is simply to do. Take a chance by doing something you've never done before. Give a chance by delegating to someone who has never done it before. Of course, you need to supervise them and make sure the whole project doesn't implode, but within reason, let them make the noncritical mistakes they can learn from.

Chapter 13

● ● ●

EMBRACE YOUR VISION AND CULTURE

To thine own self—be true.

—WILLIAM SHAKESPEARE, HAMLET

I don't make crappy movies. I spend two or three years making a film. I don't take myself seriously, but I take my movies very seriously.

—LLOYD KAUFMAN, TROMAVILLE

Willie and Lloyd are both sort of saying the same thing here. Know who you are and embrace it. Self-awareness is as important for a company as it is for each of us as an individual. There is so much talk in the business world today about culture. There are countless books, countless consultants, and countless dollars spent on "culture building" within corporations.

Often these efforts miss the core of what culture really is, what culture really means. Contrary to popular belief, culture is not about pizza and beer on Fridays, or unlimited free snacks in the company dining room (though on a film set of any size or budget, heaven help you if you don't have a functional craft-services department. The fastest way to throw any film production off course is to fail to feed the crew, and feed them well and often). At its core, culture has more to do with your brand than your office decor.

A great company culture enables and encourages employees to embody and reflect the essence of the brand in their ethic, attitude, and execution of their work. It goes deeper than office environment and is more significant than a list of core values on a whiteboard. A great company culture is one where everyone organically lives and breathes the same brand. A great culture is one where all employees understand and appreciate the DNA of the brand. They don't have to be it, but they have to believe it.

A great company culture is not a cult (though some of the highly publicized "great-culture" enterprises seem to have lost that distinction) because in a cult the disciples are most often following blindly while in a great company culture the employees are following with purpose. A great culture is created by a shared purpose that will move the company forward toward success.

Defining and communicating that purpose is core to a company's success. On a film set, the purpose is most often very clear. We are making a movie. The roadmap is the script, literally. The strategy is the production schedule. If the director is a good CEO, then everyone on set knows their role and expected contribution toward the execution of the plan and the fulfillment of the purpose.

In business, the purpose and strategy also need to be clearly defined, and as important, the role each employee plays has to be understood by the employee(s) and management. There needs to be a screenplay and a production schedule for your business.

Chapter 14

● ● ●

STRATEGIC PARTNERS: BURN HOUSES, NOT BRIDGES

Croton-on-Hudson is a lovely, quaint, and somewhat exclusive village overlooking the Hudson River in a ritzy part of Westchester County, about thirty-five minutes north of Manhattan. Lush greenery, winding roads, large picture-perfect homes, and a reasonable commute to the city make it a desirable and expensive area in which to live. Croton-on-Hudson is one of those dreamy communities that, as you drive through for the first time, your eyes and mind wander together as you imagine what it must be like to live in such an elite and peaceful hamlet. You pass the homes with tall trees and thick lawns, a luxury sedan and SUV or nice minivan parked in the driveway, and you imagine yourself in their shoes…and their clothes, and their homes and cars and country clubs for brunch on Sundays, wondering how your third Bloody Mary will impact your afternoon tennis game. Ah, Croton-on-Hudson…

So, I was a little intimidated when I entered the adorable Town Hall building for my scheduled meeting with the town supervisor to discuss my request, nay, a small favor. I was coming to ask for permission to blow up a small vacant home that was scheduled for demolition anyway. Yes, I literally asked if we could use real-live explosives and blow up a home nestled in a lovely little lakefront valley in the heart of the lovely village of Croton-on-Hudson, nestled above the lovely Hudson River.

This reminds me of one of the first business lessons I learned from my previous boss at Satori, Ernie Sauer: "If you don't ask, you don't get." Ernie said that to me in the context of me boldly asking him for a raise while dining together on my first-ever business trip abroad. I was a lowly PA (production assistant), earning $250 per week (take that, Ivy League education!) and less than a year into the job, but here we were, me, alone with the company CEO, so I went for it. And he went along, agreeing to my request, mostly because I had the gall (read "balls") to ask. After all, as he proudly espoused, "If you don't ask, you don't get."

And in the realm of independent (read "low- or no-budget") filmmaking, "If you don't ask, you don't get" is a worthy mantra for the production. Especially when it comes to scouting for shooting locations. So I asked.

"You want to do what?" said the town supervisor, now paying very close attention.

"Blow up a house that is already scheduled for demolition."

"Blow it up? With explosives?"

"Well, it would be hard to do so without explosives," I smiled and delivered the piece de resistance. "It's for a movie!"

It is truly amazing what you can get away with when you tell people "it's for a movie." *Everyone* wants to be part of making a movie and have their moment behind the scenes. Remember that church I mentioned, where we shot scenes of drugs, guns, and debauchery? Even a seasoned priest was in awe of the prospect of "lights, camera, action!" Dreams of Hollywood are deeply imprinted in the minds of most humans. Powerfully imprinted, so deeply that intelligent, sane, hardworking individuals can be mesmerized and bedazzled into confusing Tromaville for Hollywood and letting the likes of our literal motley crew and me wreak havoc on their homes and businesses, temporarily turning lives and livelihoods inside out, all in the name of "cinema!" And, in the case of Indy productions like ours, all for no compensation (other than the glory of the experience).

As the wide-eyed Croton-on-Hudson town supervisor pondered my polite pyrotechnic request, I figured I might as well go for broke.

"We'd also like your local fire department to be on hand to put out the raging inferno after the building goes boom. OK? And we have no budget for any of this (except, of course, the explosives…we have a budget for that). So, what do you say?"

To break the awkward silence, I added, "And the fire department can use this as a great training experience—a controlled explosion for them to put out…a valuable opportunity for sure."

And boom! That was the clincher that made our big boom possible. The town supervisor got it all approved. Of course, there were permits and insurance and other details to be worked out, but we came to them with the blessing of the NY Governor's Film Commission, who had supplied us with the list of "scheduled demolitions" that led us to Croton-on-Hudson in the first place.

Which begs me to mention the value of city and state film commissions. They are populated by hardworking and dedicated film-loving staff that are there to help you, struggling filmmaker, regardless of your pedigree or budget. All you have to do is ask. Long before Lloyd's lovely and talented wife Pattie Pie (er, I mean Patricia) was appointed to head the NY State Governor's Film Commission, the Troma Team was wise enough to leverage the free resources of the New York City, New York State, and New Jersey Film Commissions. Are there similar state or city funded resources to assist you in your industry? Dig in. You might be surprised.

Back to our big blast in Croton-on-Hudson. It was, indeed, a blast. The weather was perfect. The fire department ready and eager to engage in their "training exercise," and of course, our cast and crew were equally fired up to start production of *The Toxic Avenger Part II* with a bang!

Croton-on-Hudson got their building demolished as planned. Plus, their fire department had an exemplary training opportunity. And to top it all off, the Troma Team got a great location, and an even better explosion, all on film, and all for free.

The Big Boom (Screen capture from *The Toxic Avenger Part II*)

Chapter 15

● ● ●

IF YOU DON'T WANT TO SWALLOW A FROG, START WITH A STUNT

There's a popular productivity quote that is often attributed to Mark Twain about swallowing a live frog every morning. If you can get past that rather grotesque task, then anything else the day may bring on should seem infinitely more manageable. The fate of the poor frog aside, the concept is one we embraced when making movies in Tromaville, and it is a sound practice for any business. Start with the hard stuff.

When making a movie, especially a low-budget action/horror flick, the hard stuff is typically anything involving stunts or special effects. Those are the days that cost more money, often take more time, and ultimately have more at stake because it is harder to "fix it in editing" should the planned stunt go awry on film. These were the pre-CGI[1] days, and things like explosions and crazy car stunts were all done "live" on film for the most part. When we blew up a building, there were real explosives, fire, and debris. Cameras were set behind protective plexiglass shields, and crew and actors were reduced to the bare minimum possible and kept as far away from potential harm as possible. Fun stuff. Exciting stuff.

---

1. "CGI" referring to computer-generated imagery—that is, the technology behind digital effects. The only "digital" effects available to Troma at the time were effects involving fingers and toes.

Dangerous stuff. So why not do it on the very first day of filming, before anyone is comfortable working with each other?

Swallow the frog.

Exactly.

Do some really super hard shit right at the beginning to get everyone focused (and maybe a little nervous), but in truth, there's no better way to quickly bond a group of disparate people than to have them accomplish a really hard, potentially dangerous, task together. Focus is required. Teamwork is required. It is going from zero to sixty in the first few hours of working together. It forces the cream to rise to the top and quickly exposes the weak links in the chain. (There were always fewer people on the crew on day two than there were on day one.) It is risky, but it is also rewarding. And when it works (actually more often than not), it sets the tone for the rest of the production, with everyone diving in with a level of confidence and camaraderie that otherwise might have taken weeks to develop.

So, pretty much every Troma production I worked on started with a bang—literally and figuratively.

Are you pulling a team together for a project? Try scheduling the equivalent of your explosion or stunt right up front. Put the team to the test. Swallow the frog. (Then spit it out so the Troma Team can use it as a prop in that tender love scene that requires a regurgitated amphibian.)

Chapter 16

● ● ●

REPURPOSE, ON PURPOSE

As stunts go, we did some amazing ones at Troma, and the best of them, like the dramatic (and now infamous) "car flip" have been used and reused in countless Troma movies. Shot one quiet afternoon on the back streets of Hoboken, New Jersey, while costly and complicated to shoot, the "car flip" has perhaps become the most cost-effective bit of film ever shot by the Troma Team (when amortized across the vast number of subsequent films the same sequence has appeared in). Why not? It's a great stunt, even the seventeenth time you see it. Like a fine wine, it gets fermented—er, I mean better—with age. Like the pestering of a wild and crazy two-year-old toddler, with repetition, it becomes less annoying and cuter. Like a pimple that, after it won't go away for nine months, reinvents itself as a beauty mark. You get the idea.

Of course, in the case of Troma, given the cult and culture of the rabid fan base, repurposing a stunt or scene across multiple movies turns into a welcome wink to the knowing film fan who can spot the repeated spot. So not only does the cloned scene save time and money, it becomes an Easter egg that delights eagle-eyed fans who are paying close attention—a double whammy win for the Troma Team.

What content can you wisely repurpose for your purposes? Do you have anything that can double as an Easter egg to charm your customers?

Chapter 17

● ● ●

ALWAYS SALUTE THE SCHWAG

"I pledge allegiance to the schwag…of the United States of Tromaville." As part of the Troma Team, I quickly learned the power of "schwag" and the importance of always "carrying." In this instance carrying did not mean a concealed weapon, although one could argue that good schwag is an excellent sales and marketing weapon. In Tromaville carrying meant you were always equipped with a supply of stuff—stickers, flyers, T-shirts—schwag. Your briefcase was full of the stuff. If you owned a car, your trunk was full of the stuff. If you carried a purse or murse,[2] your purse or murse was full of the stuff. While representing the Troma Team, you never walked into a meeting empty handed. You *always* had your schwag at the ready. Schwag sells.

There's a reason printed paper flyers were called "sell sheets" in the movie business. They were also called "slicks," perhaps because the slicker they were, the better they sold. For every movie in the Troma library, having a great key art image that became the basis of the poster, and then the smaller sell sheets, was essential. As essential as having a good trailer. Arguably far more essential than having a good movie. Back in the day, especially in the realm of international film distribution, the

---

2. A "murse" is a man-purse, carried by a man, just as a "manzier" is a brazier worn by a man. Watch *Seinfeld* reruns for more details.

sale (technically, the licensing) of a film for distribution to a small foreign market was often concluded based on the sell sheet and trailer alone, many times long before the film in question had actually been completed (or in some cases, even started). We were selling the dream. Selling the outcome. And schwag helped.

Like trusty Boy and Girl Scouts, always carrying schwag meant you were always prepared. You never knew when you'd have the opportunity to leave behind that flyer for *Curse of the Cannibal Confederates* or that gorgeous green "I love Toxie" sticker. And then there were the T-shirts. Especially the T-shirts. We would print bright-red (and sometimes yellow) "I made the Troma Team" T-shirts by the hundreds. They were inexpensive thin cotton tees with a big Troma logo on them, and people loved them. When it came to production time, our "I-Made-the-Troma-Team" tees were like a liquid currency. They were our beads, our wampum, our bitcoin, and often our savior. It is amazing what regular unassuming humans will do or give up in exchange for a free T-shirt.

When scouting for locations, popping open the car trunk and tossing a couple of T-shirts to the owner of the property you are begging to trample and defame was often the tipping point that sealed the deal. When casting dozens of background actors (we never had extras…always "background actors") to fill a scene, hordes of fans would stand for long grueling days, all for a stale bagel at seven in the morning and a Troma T-shirt when they left at the end of the day, often past midnight.

When making a movie, especially a low-budget independent movie, there are 1,000 things that can go wrong at any moment. Giving someone a free T-shirt can solve 937 of them.

As proof that the Troma Team always carries (schwag) wherever they go, I will share a story that Hertz. Not Herz as in Michael Herz, Lloyd's partner in cinematic crime and Troma cofounder, but rather Hertz as in the car rental company that doesn't quite try as hard as Avis. Many years after I emigrated from Tromaville, I was in Los Angeles on business, and I rented a car there. At one point while navigating my way through the tortuous traffic that is synonymous with driving in LA, I stopped short at a light, my unpracticed foot a bit heavy on the brakes of the unfamiliar vehicle. As I screeched to a sudden stop, a sudden mess of papers and folders slid out from under the driver's seat. I looked down, and lo and behold, my feet were surrounded by Troma schwag—flyers, stickers, press kits, and the like. It was literally a blast from the past.

I laughed, and at the first opportunity I called Lloyd asking him if he had recently been in LA. "I just got back last night," he replied. "How did you know?"

"Did you rent a car there?" I queried.

"Of course, I did; it's LA," said Lloyd. (This was years ago, before the invasion of Uber).

"Well, I think I rented the same car you were driving. You left your schwag under the front seat!"

Yep. He did.

Schwag rules.

Chapter 18

● ● ●

PLAYING BY THE RULES

By now you may be thinking that things were fairly loosey-goosey in Tromaville, with inexperienced young lads and lasses running wild and wreaking havoc. You would be mostly correct. In truth, while there were certainly some wild and crazy times (and even more wild and crazy characters and personalities), much of the working of the Troma machine was actually quite well-oiled. There were processes and procedures, and there were rules. In particular, there were the "Rules of Production."

On every Troma movie set, in numerous, highly visible locations, the following sign was always posted:

Rules of Production:

1. Safety to people
2. Safety to property
3. Make a good film!

This was key. This was important. These were the rules Troma lived by on set, and at any given moment, Lloyd could walk up to a member of the cast or crew and quiz them on these three simple rules, and they had better know them. When it came to setiquette (etiquette on the set), the Troma Team was very clear on their priorities. A film set can be a dangerous place. There are lights, there are cameras, and there is action—big heavy things that can fall on people, miles of cables and electrical cords strewn about, vehicles, explosives, and lots of people around. A lot can go wrong. A lot does go wrong. It is a tribute to the dedication to these three "rules of production" that in over forty years and dozens of productions, Troma has a solid record and reputation when it comes to safety.

Safety to people is the number one priority. Safety to property is second. We were grateful for the fair deals we received on the equipment we borrowed or rented. We were forever grateful for the folks who generously let us use their homes and businesses as sets and locations for filming. The least we could do was to respect their property and do all we could to leave it in the same condition it was in when we arrived (which, frankly, was often no small task).

Finally, the third rule was to "make a good film" and in practice, if you paid attention to the first two rules, you were far more likely to succeed on the third.

These were good lessons in focus and culture. While a Troma film set consisted of a wild and varied sampling of human existence, a seemingly random collection of delightfully disparate souls, the one thing that they all had to have in common was respect for and adherence to the "Rules of Production." Anyone who could not live up to these three simple concepts did not belong (and did not last long).

While in some cases, rules can be restrictive, when they are simple, direct, and core to your objective, a few good rules can help bind your team together and help keep things moving forward in a positive way. If it can work for Troma, it can work for you.

What are your business's "rules of production"?

Chapter 19

● ● ●

FIX IT, OR FORGET IT...FAST

On a movie set, there is no shortage of things that can go wrong. Your camera truck can be stolen. Your location can be locked when you arrive with the owner completely denying they ever gave you permission to come and film there. Your lead actress can refuse to come out of the bathroom to film a scene or refuse to kiss the leading monster—er, man, despite the romantic scene that was in the script and agreed to when she was hired. Essential costumes and props disappear. Cars containing essential talent or equipment break down. It rains (it pours). Actors show up drunk. Actors show up without knowing their lines. Actors don't show up. Assholes do show up. Equipment breaks. Crew members quit. Sound people forget to record. Camera people forget to load film. It rains (it pours). Teamsters protest and interfere. Stunts don't work as planned. You run out of power. You run out of light. You run out of time. You run out of money. You run out screaming.

Shit happens.

Lots of shit.

Every day.

All the time.

It is fun, really.

That's Hollywood (well, Tromaville).

But on a set, the clock is always ticking, and whether you are on a shoestring Indy budget or a gazillion-dollar studio budget, time is still money. There are pages to cover, and a schedule to follow. The shit may hit the fan, but the film still needs to end up in the can. So, when something does go wrong, and it will, you need to make a decision. You need to fix it, fast, or work around it, fast. Innovation and creativity will save the day more than money will, and that's a solid lesson for any business.

Even if you have the money, replacing something that breaks can take time and delay production. What's the backup plan? To successfully make a B-movie, you'd better always have a plan B (and frankly, the same applies even if you are attempting to make a blockbuster).

Do you have a true plan B for your business? When making a movie, learning to be prepared and expect the unexpected is essential (which actually makes the unexpected the expected).

Filming on a soundstage is expensive and outside the budget of most independent films. As a result, to get great on-screen production values at a reasonable cost, many Indy films are shot "on location," leveraging the scenic beauty of the real world in lieu of the fabricated beauty and control of a costly studio set. But in the real world, you can't control Mother Nature, and your location is always at risk of being shut down by bad weather. Having a plan B means that for every day of exterior filming, you had better have an alternate scene ready to be shot indoors should Mother Nature decide to fool you for a change. That means an alternative location, indoors and nearby, so you could quickly and efficiently save the day.

So, when we were filming *The Toxic Avenger Part II* (and *Part III*) in and around the lovely town of Peekskill, NY, we always had several indoor "sets" ready and waiting inside the abandoned Masonic temple that doubled as our local production office. While these makeshift sets were far from "studio" quality, they were good enough, and if Mother Nature decided to poop on our heads, without hesitation we knew exactly what to do, where to go, and how to make the day as productive as possible.

This is a lesson that is easy to forget in the nonmovie world because in most businesses there is a lot more flexibility on a day-to-day basis than there is on a movie set. You may be under pressure to meet a monthly or quarterly goal, but what about losing sunlight before all the necessary pages are shot in a location you absolutely, positively can never return to after the end of the day? Movies function day to day, and that fosters a discipline that would be beneficial to apply to any business. Every day on set must contribute to the end-goal of a finished film.

Is every day at your office contributing to your end-goal? It's hard, and something I try to remind myself of, not always successfully.

Chapter 20

● ● ●

THIS MEANS *WAR*

They say "business is war." I am not sure who "they" are, but I can assure you that when I began getting involved in Troma's business, my first shot at working on a movie was indeed war. Literally. The very first Troma film I had the opportunity to work on was *Troma's War*. When I enlisted, my job at Troma was to sell movies, but I dreamed of making them. When plans began for *Troma's War*, my number came up, and I was drafted to "temporarily" move over from sales to production. My dream had come true, and like many dreams we have, be careful what you wish for—you might get it.

If you haven't yet had the pleasure and delight of seeing *Troma's War*, it is the story of a plane crash on a mysterious island long before the TV series *Lost* laid claim to similar territory. Rather than the long-unfulfilled, and unexplained, "monsters" of the TV series, the lost crash survivors in *Troma's War* find themselves on an island run by bizarre and deadly terrorists. According to *Variety*, *Troma's War* "makes *Rambo III* look like *Lassie Come Home*!" It was quite an entrée into filmmaking for me.

Yes, I wanted to make movies. No, I had no freakin' idea what that meant, especially in Tromaville. One moment I was trying to sell *Rabid Grannies* to a home-video distributor in Japan, and the next moment I was on my way to Camp Smith, training ground for the NY Army National Guard, outside Peekskill, NY, to meet with Colonel Garvey to see if I could convince him to let us use their grounds to film and blow shit up (and let our kooky cast and crew live in their barracks for weeks at a time). The irony of having the cast and crew of *Troma's War* live and film on a military base was not lost on any of us.

But let's start by looking at how the *War* began.

Once there's a script and a budget and funds to cover said budget (or enough of the promise of funds, through presales and other means, to risk taking the risk of pulling the trigger on the production), it is time to start staffing up and commencing "preproduction." Preproduction is the planning stage for a movie production when the script is broken down into manageable daily chunks, and the schedule is set. The locations are scouted and finalized, cast and crew are hired, and costumes and props are decided upon and created. Basically, everything and anything you can do in advance of actual filming so that you are ready to go like a well-oiled machine when that first day of "Principal Photography" rolls around.

Sounds great, right? Of course, it is never as smooth as the previous few sentences make it sound, and come day one of filming that ideal well-oiled machine may well spit and sputter like an aged clunker only partially restored. Still, it can and must move forward. The proverbial clock is ticking, and, like the car you drive around in the midst of rebuilding it, you can keep working on the film machine while it is running. Not ideal, but not unusual, especially for a low-budget Indy production, where location and talent availability might dictate a hard start date. Ready or not, here we come!

As we started hiring (and given the lack of actual monetary compensation offered to many early staffers I am using the term "hiring" lightly), we needed to set up a temporary production office to act as home base, ideally somewhere nearby (but definitely not in) the Troma Building. We found a great deal on a short-term lease on a dinky and dirty four-story, walk-up brownstone on West Forty-Eighth Street, a short walk from Tromaville central. I remember thinking it was an odd building with an odd smell, and odd-looking "cubicles," each curtained off and just wide enough for a small mattress to fit inside. Oh, and did I mention that there was a red light by the front door stoop?

Admittedly, I was quite naive in those days, and it took me a few late nights in the production office (where some of our young, more adventurous Troma Team members had essentially moved in) before I realized why this building was "available" so inexpensively. I figured it out when every night an odd "gentleman" or two would ring the doorbell only to be awkwardly surprised when one of our heavily pierced and tattooed young folks of indiscriminate gender would answer the door. The "gentlemen" would invariably look past the welcoming Tromite as if they were hoping to see a familiar face inside, and then, clearly disappointed that they did not, would turn and hurriedly leave, mumbling obscenities under their alcohol-laced breath. Yep, our production office had previously been an operating brothel. Oh, brothel, er, oh brother! When the realization dawned on me, I felt truly blessed that I had a home to retreat to each night and was not one of the "adventurous ones" camping out on the "great mattresses" the previous tenants had left behind.

Despite its lewd history, our production office for *Troma's War* served its purpose, and our preproduction was off and running, and I was learning on the fly. I went to battle in *Troma's War*, and it was my deployment to film school…on steroids. But the lessons I learned in preparation, scheduling, and negotiation, were lessons that have proven to be valuable in every career move I've made since. The discipline and planning of preproduction is something that every product launch could benefit from. Few businesses understand their processes as well as a film production, where literally every page of the script (think product roadmap) is broken down into manageable (well, hopefully manageable) chunks, to be executed according to a strict schedule, literally laid out on a schedule board for all to see. Imagine how much more efficient your business would be if it were broken down with the detail and depth even a lowly Troma production had. Every day was fully accounted for, with a breakdown of every needed element—location, actors, costumes, set pieces, props, equipment, crew, a plan to get us all there, a plan to shoot something else should Mother Nature, or other forces, interfere.

Of course, things were fluid and could and would change along the way, but at the onset, we had a plan that, in theory, would successfully get us from point A to point B. From having nothing to having all the necessary footage in the can to piece together the film we intended to make.

Do you have a script breakdown for your business?

Chapter 21

● ● ●

DELEGATE OR DIE

One thing that is very clear about making a movie is that it is a collaborative art. Other than for a very few, very rare exceptions, making a film means working with a team. Even the smallest production has actors, crew, and a director at the least. Unlike writing or painting or sculpting, where your art can truly be the pursuit of a sole proprietor, making a movie is almost always a collaboration, and more often than not, puts OPM (other people's money) at risk. That means pressure to perform.

Such that it is a collaborative art, the fine art of effective delegation becomes an invaluable skill for a filmmaker. The "auteur" theory notwithstanding, when making a film you really cannot do everything yourself. The best filmmakers recognize this and surround themselves with outstanding talent, from the DP and cinematographer to the actors and actresses, the grips and sound people, as well as the costume and set designers, and every other department head. In truth, the best directors don't need to know how to do everything themselves, but rather they need to know how to surround themselves with the folks who do know everything, and they need to be an effective commander in chief, smartly delegating the tasks necessary to achieve their particular vision for the film.

No small task, but a great business lesson.

Too many entrepreneurs think they can and must do everything themselves. That might work when they are a bootstrapped team of two founders, but as soon as you take in your first Angel round or Series A, you have an obligation to your investors and no longer just to yourself and your "vision."

Understanding how to delegate is perhaps the most valuable thing an entrepreneur can learn. Doing everything yourself does not scale. Being able to delegate well is akin to being able to lead well, and frankly, to being able to get shit done. And effective delegation is not easy. When it comes to managing a team, there is no such thing as "set it and forget it." Just because you have assigned a task to someone doesn't mean you have absolved yourself from it. As the director (i.e., "the boss") you are ultimately responsible for it all, regardless of who actually executed the task. If all goes awry, it is you who should (and will) get executed (alongside your loyal, but ineffective, lieutenants). A good filmmaker, like a good businessperson, knows to "inspect what they expect" and monitor and check up on the tasks they have assigned to others.

On a movie set, it is not uncommon to have a short meeting with department heads late at night, to review the schedule for the next day and ensure, while there is still time to make adjustments, that everything delegated has been taken care of and is ready to go for the morning and day ahead.

This kind of department-head huddle is a good practice for any business. Check in and check up, to avoid having to check out!

Chapter 22

● ● ●

LOCATION, LOCATION, LOCATION

War is hell. And the hell of *Troma's War*, according to the script, begins with a horrific, fiery plane crash onto a deserted tropical island. So, all we needed to recreate such a scene was a beautiful, desolate beach, with no hint of civilization. Oh, and of course we would need to "dress" such a pristine and lovely beach with the smoldering remains of a commercial passenger aircraft, post-crash. Easy, right? As it turned out, thanks to the terrific support of the NY State Governor's Film Commission (again, many years before Lloyd's wife Pat would be appointed to head said commission), we were told about a little-known property of the state, on the north shore of Long Island, Caumsett State Park.

Once owned by Marshall Field III and purchased by the State of New York in 1961, the beach at the park was situated on a peninsula, Lloyd Neck (coincidence? I think not) that jutted out into the Long Island sound in such a way that you could create a view where no buildings or lights were visible. Just unobstructed water and hilly beach, with trees along the edges of the sand. It was perfect, but it was complicated. There was nothing in the area where we needed to film. No buildings, no structures, no electricity or bathrooms or phones. At least three miles from anything even resembling civilization. Visually perfect and a logistic nightmare. Not only would we have to get cast, crew, equipment, and props there (and back) but we had night filming on the schedule and a wide range of required environmental rules and guidelines we'd have to adhere to in order to keep the location in the same condition as we found it. Still, the location was perfect (and, as a state-owned property, the price was right...zippo, as long as we arranged for the proper permits).

Troma's War was essentially shot on two primary locations: Caumsett State Park on Long Island and Camp Smith in Peekskill, NY. Both locations were handed to us courtesy of the NY State Governor's Film Commission, an invaluable resource for an independent production such as ours. Our set department managed to get hold of airplane doors and pieces of fuselage and other airplane parts such that we truly made the once-pristine beach look like an actual crash site. The natural beauty of the location created production values that far exceeded our budget and made *Troma's War* one of the best-looking Troma films to date when it was released. The woods on the edges of the beach blended well with the woods of Camp Smith creating a realistic and believable deserted island setting as, in the finished film, we seamlessly move back and forth between the two distinct (and distinctly different) locales. Essentially, everything on the beach was shot at Caumsett State Park, and everything in the woods was shot at Camp Smith. When actors are seen stepping into the woods from the beach, they were essentially then teleporting themselves to the woods of Camp Smith. Ahh, the magic of the cinema...

As one can glean from the title, *Troma's War* involved lots of battles (and I am not just referring to the arguments between Lloyd, Michael, and myself...one of which drove me to quit. But I returned, and I digress). The script called for lots of action, guns, and explosions. Pyrotechnics was practically a supporting actor based on the number of scenes that called for explosions and blasts. Fortunately, we had the services of the soft-spoken Will Caban, aptly nicknamed "Will Kaboom," to handle the more explosive pages of the script. Will was quiet, calm, and completely dedicated to his craft of blowing things to kingdom come. He drove around in a nondescript, beat-up brown panel van loaded with mortars and mounds of flammable and explosive materials. I could not imagine today how he could do what he did then, but I always admired him as a man who truly had a blast at work.

The weapons of *War* were another challenge as the script called for a very well-armed militia of terrorist baddies and near-constant gunfights. Renting realistic stage guns, including heavy arms and automatic weapons, along with the requisite rounds of noisy, flash-firing "blanks," can be a costly and complicated proposition. As much as the actual rental of such equipment was a big deal, as weapons were needed just about every day, we'd need a near full-time weapons wrangler to manage, secure, and clean all the weapons, as well as train our actors and actresses in the proper and safe use of the arsenal. As it turned out, the owner of NY's best modern theatrical gun collection was also an accomplished actor in his own right, and so not only did we rent his guns, buy his ammunition, and hire him as their daily wrangler but we also cast Rick Washburn in one of the lead roles. If he had to be on the set every day to handle the weapons anyway, we might as well use him in front of the camera too. And we did.

Lesson learned: Find out the hidden talents of your teammates, and explore how they can use their passions to further your cause. Just as we were able to leverage Rick Washburn, the actor, to maximize his contribution as more than just the weapons guy, what are the talents of your team that can be utilized? Do you have budding photographers and videographers among your midst? Wouldn't they love to show off their talents to benefit the company rather than have you hire some outsider to do something they are already passionate about? Your best contractors and evangelists could already be in your midst. Give them a chance to shine in an area they weren't necessarily hired for. What do you think?

With the near-daily requirement of shooting off weapons and blowing stuff up, we needed a location that would allow such things. Not every neighborhood would welcome such noisy violence as easily as Croton-on-Hudson took to our explosive home demolition. And besides, the blast we had at Croton-on-Hudson was a year or so after *Troma's War* was over. But Camp Smith was perfect! As a military training facility, the sound of artillery fire and explosions were de rigueur. They even had their own on-site fire department to handle the aftermath of Mr. Caban's kabooms. The Colonel and his staff could not have been more accommodating, and the woods and grounds of Camp Smith became our home away from home for the majority of the filming of *Troma's War*.

In truth, the two locations, Caumsett State Park and Camp Smith, played a substantial role in the success of the film (and by Troma standards, the war was won, and *Troma's War* was a success). It was also the early and growing days of home video, and *Troma's War* was first in a series of well-publicized Troma VHS releases by Media Home Entertainment, one of the leaders in the then-nascent home-video industry.

Scouting for and securing filming locations was by far one of my favorite aspects of making movies, and the skills and experiences handling such negotiations are some of the most valuable I've carried forward throughout my career. Relationships, sincerity, authenticity, and directness were the keys to successfully securing locations like Camp Smith and Caumsett State Park. We were upfront about our needs and the content we were creating, and we were upfront about our respect for the process and responsibility to care for the people and property under our watch (remember the "Rules of Production").

Chapter 23

● ● ●

EVERYONE IS EXPENDABLE (ESPECIALLY IF YOU WEAR A MASK)

Dealing with "talent" is a special skill in and of itself. Like it or not, "talent" is special, and often for the best results, you need to treat them special. Fortunately, by the time I made it to Tromaville, I had a good sense of this, having produced the early cable TV show *Celebrity* when I worked at Satori. The hostess of that show was the great NY disc jockey Alison "The Nightbird" Steele. When I worked with Alison, she was already a celebrity in her own right, one of the first female FM radio DJ's to make it big on the prestigious NY City Classic Rock station, WNEW. For the show, we often had to show up at various hotels to interview famous actors and actresses in town to promote their latest movies. Everyone, from Jane Fonda to Robin Williams, to Christopher Reeve, and countless other A-list stars of the day.

Alison was a pro, and wonderful to work with, but she had one quirk. She was always late. Always. We were typically on a tight interview schedule as the stars were basically on a junket conducting back-to-back interviews all day long, so we needed to show up and be ready to go at our appointed slot. Difficult to do with Alison's chronic tardiness. So, we began to adjust her call time to account for this. If our interview was scheduled to begin at 9:00 a.m. and she needed thirty minutes to get ready, we'd tell Alison that her call time was 8:00 a.m. Invariably she'd show up at 8:30 a.m., and we'd be on time for the 9:00 a.m. shoot. This worked like a charm until one day she actually showed up "on time" and saw that we were just sitting around doing nothing because we had plenty of time to set up. She figured out our game, and we could never play it again. Talent.

Back in Tromaville, we had our own set of talent issues, from on-set relationships gone awry, to drinking issues, and on and on. Often what was most challenging was what I'd call "prima donna syndrome"—when our stars became star struck with themselves. It turns out that actors and actresses don't have to be paid huge sums to think and act like a star (or, more accurately, their warped personal vision of how a "real" star might behave). Even in the context of a low-budget action/horror film, the stars want to be treated as such. Those of us on the production side, if we wanted to keep the set moving and on schedule, often needed to swallow our pride, roll our eyes (when nobody was looking), and suck up to the whims of those with the most screen time. To a point.

And then there was Toxie.

The titular role in *The Toxic Avenger* is, of course, the Toxic Avenger himself, affectionately known as "Toxie." Mind you that the actor (and, as you'll soon see, actors) who portrayed Toxie on film all had one very crucial thing in common: they wore a freakin' mask over their heads! The popular hideously deformed creature of superhuman size and strength, the first superhero from New Jersey, the goofy guy who emerged from a vat of toxic chemicals, was always played by an actor wearing a full-head mask, not makeup. Other than the whites of their eyes and teeth, essentially there was no individually identifiable part of the actor's face or features visible when they were in front of the camera as Toxie. Toxie was the star. The actor(s) in the costume and mask were, for all intents and purposes, anonymous. This came in handy in a number of ways.

First of all, when we decided to create a sequel to *The Toxic Avenger*, we didn't have to worry about trying to dig up the dude who played Toxie in the original film. We could cast any muscular mensch we wanted and have them fill our hero's goo-soled shoes.

Having Toxie's presence dictated by the presence of virtually anyone wearing the mask had many other efficiencies. In particular, while the real Toxie was filming one scene, a second unit could be off shooting stunts or effects with Toxie at the same time. All we needed was to have duplicate masks and costumes, and the stunt teams and effects teams were ready to rock and roll, with one of their own dressed as Toxie. From a production perspective, it was super-efficient. From the point of view of the actor playing the primary Toxie it was super annoying. In his mask-covered mind, he was the star. He should be the only one in front of the camera in his hideously deformed glory.

So, as we set out to make the sequel to *The Toxic Avenger*, we hired a well-muscled hunk to play the infamous lead role. I'll call him John (mostly because his name was John, and because, smart as you are, I know you'll just look at the publicly available film credits and figure it out!) John was indeed a great Toxie until he got a bit too full of himself. While he never went so far as to demand that there would be no brown M&M's on set, he did start to make things difficult as his case of "prima donna syndrome" kicked into high gear. Eventually, Toxie John became his own worst enemy, and we mutually decided it was time for us to go our separate ways. Fortunately, seeing the proverbial writing on the wall, we had already been integrating Toxie's backup, who I'll call Ron (mostly because his name was Ron, and because, smart as you are, I know you'll just look at the publicly available film credits and figure it out!) By the time John moved on, Ron was all set to be the primary Toxie.

So, if you watch carefully, in *The Toxic Avenger Part II* and *III*, you can spot the physical differences between Toxie John and Toxie Ron, in height and musculature, but Toxie is such a strong character that his heart and soul stands out and rings true, regardless of who the man is behind the mask, and the film plays on just fine.

Everyone is expendable.
Even me and you.
Don't worry about it, but don't forget it either.

Chapter 24

● ● ●

BE OPEN TO THE UNEXPECTED

You never know where inspiration will come from. The key is to be open to seeing it and acting upon it when it decides to burst in on you unexpectedly.

Back in the days when our cars were not actually computers on wheels, there was a fad when anyone with a child would stick a suction cupped diamond-shaped yellow sign to the window of their car that said "Baby on board," the idea being that other drivers would be more careful driving around a car that was transporting a young, defenseless human. Parents loved it, and the signs became a literal sign of the times. You'd see them stuck inside vehicle windows everywhere. Whoever came up with those signs was making serious bank. And of course, the more popular they became, the riper they became for being copied and parodied. Soon, as an attempt to deter would-be robbers, some cars started posting the same yellow diamond sign that said "No radio on board."

There's a running visual joke throughout *Sgt. Kabukiman NYPD*, where a parked car is broken into, and then we see it has one of the "No radio on board" signs, in this case presumably left by the lowlifes who just broke in and stole the car's radio. Throughout the film, we revisit the car as more things are stolen, and more yellow suction cup signs are added to the window. Eventually, we see the car, up on blocks, stripped bare, with a "No tires on board" sign added to the crowded windows. Hahaha. Corny but timely (those yellow suction cup signs were really a thing).

Whether you thought the car gag was funny or not, there's a story behind how it ended up in the script. Lloyd and I were writing the screenplay for *Sgt. Kabukiman NYPD* at his place on the Upper East Side. As we sat in the small room (the former closet that was now "the computer room" so we could type our script in bits and bytes), we were interrupted by the persistent shrill piercing sound of a car alarm. Any excuse to not write was welcome, so we stopped what we were doing (or not doing) and gathered by the second-story window.

There, on the street below us, we watched the dude who had just smashed the window of the car parked on the street in front of the Kaufmans' humble abode. It was summer time, hot, and the window was already half-way open to welcome the occasional breeze. Instinctively we screamed out the window in unison, "Hey! Get away from that car!" Startled, the would-be car thief looked up at us and started to run. Without hesitation, Lloyd and I looked at each other, turned, and bounded down the stairs and out the front door onto the street. A quick glance at the smashed car window and requisite glass on the curb beside, and another glance down the street toward the corner where our culprit could be seen running from the scene.

Perhaps it was because we were in the midst of writing the story of a crime-fighting New York City cop who turns into a crime-fighting, kimono-wearing superhero, or perhaps because we were just a couple of nerdy idiots, but whatever reason we felt compelled to run down the block screaming "stop, thief!" Needless to say, the thief did not stop. The jaded New Yorkers around us looked at us as if we were indeed a couple of nerdy idiots. Huffing and puffing from our brief, unexpected bout of cardiovascular activity, we put our tails between our legs and dejectedly walked back to Lloyd's. We were clearly not effective crime-fighters in real life. So we trudged back up the stairs to the computer closet and our screenplay in progress and memorialized the experience by writing in the aforementioned car gag.

Inspiration comes in many forms and often in unexpected shapes and sizes. You need to be ready to see it, and embrace it (even if doing so makes you appear to be a nerdy idiot).

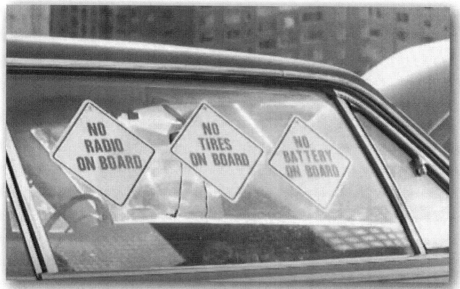

No tires on board! (Screen capture from *Sgt. Kabukiman NYPD*)

Chapter 25

● ● ●

INFLUENCING THE INFLUENCERS

One of the amazing things about Troma is the incredible impact Lloyd, Michael, and the Troma Team have had on today's mainstream film industry. Because of the general lack of respect for Troma's inimitable style of moviemaking, the deep influence it has had has gone largely unnoticed by the public at large. In fact, I should not say Troma's "inimitable" style because indeed it has been imitated by Hollywood proper many, many times (see the original *Robocop* for one example). Yet more than the on-screen talent that has passed through Tromaville (the likes of Kevin Costner, Marisa Tomei, Vincent D'Onofrio, Samuel L. Jackson, Billy Bob Thornton, and many others) perhaps the greatest influence is the impact Troma has had on some of today's most well-known and well-respected filmmakers.

As a young Tromite myself, I witnessed many of these soon-to-be-greats come by to visit Troma at our office or at an industry event to pay homage to Lloyd and Michael and catch a bit of the "Eau du Troma" in person. The Troma suite at the Carlton Hotel during the annual Cannes Film Festival or our hotel room office at the annual American Film Market in Los Angeles were both particularly popular hangouts for the soon-to-be-famous filmmakers.

Like the time a scruffy kid from New Zealand came by the Troma suite in Cannes. He professed his Troma fandom and hung out to talk with Lloyd about his film, which we had seen and admired, and which he said was influenced by his admiration for Troma. The film in question was aptly named *Bad Taste* (after all, it was inspired by Troma). Oh, and the scruffy filmmaker from New Zealand? His name was (and still is) Peter Jackson. Yes, that Peter "Lord of The Rings" Jackson. Others who would visit with us in Cannes in the early days of their budding careers included Quentin Tarantino, another loyal fan. And then there are filmmakers who were groomed in Tromaville.

After I left Tromaville in 1994, a young, educated lad was hired, ostensibly to replace me. His name was (and still is) James Gunn. James cowrote *Tromeo and Juliet* with Lloyd, and of course has gone on to become one of the greatest directors of our time, helming, among other films, the megasuccessful Marvel/Disney epic *Guardians of the Galaxy*. Other bigwigs who have collaborated with Troma include *South Park* creators Trey Parker and Matt Stone. Before they created one of the most successful musicals in Broadway history, *Book of Mormon*, their early film *Cannibal! The Musical* was released by the Troma Team.

So what is it about Troma that so influences the influencers? I think it boils down to a culture, creativity, and freedom that many filmmakers and creatives find genuinely inspiring. And a great deal of credit goes to Lloyd and Michael, and especially Lloyd as the more visible face of Troma (if you don't count Toxie's hideously deformed face). To filmmaker-fans, Troma represents the embodiment of the independent auteur. Lloyd and Michael created a world for themselves where they are beholden to no one and can make any film, and any creative choices they want. It could be bizarre, it could be silly, it could be funny, it could be gory, it could be all of the above. Most of all, if they are willing to create it, it can be— without the interference and baggage that normally comes with making a movie.

Lloyd and Michael are a quirky pair. They met at Yale. Michael went on to NYU Law School. Lloyd studied Chinese in college and spoke fluent Mandarin decades before it became both a fashionable and profitable pursuit. Somehow, Lloyd, this educated and erudite, bow-tie-wearing, sometime socialite, Upper East Side son of a successful attorney had a predilection for creating goofy, often cheesy (dare I say schlocky) and often violent and bloody, yet somehow very human, films. And he convinced his equally smart and strongly business-minded Yale buddy to join him in a venture that became a forty-plus-year adventure. It's like the very first time the Reese's folks put chocolate and peanut butter together. Who knew? The quirky combo and quirkier tastes of Lloyd Kaufman and Michael Herz became an object of admiration to some, and even jealousy to others.

There are plenty of folks in Hollywood who made more money than Troma did. But there are few, if any, that have had a career with the real creative freedom Lloyd and Michael enjoy and the ability to say "no" to anything that did not suit their muse of the moment. They are also very transparent and very humble. While the Troma Team really does take the business of making movies seriously, they never take themselves too seriously. They are fully aware that almost everything they do is done with at least somebody's ripped-out tongue held firmly in cheek. That self-deprecating and honest approach has proven to be very appealing. And not just to the filmmaking community and fans, but also to the media.

Given the genre of gory, silly, low-budget and often low-brow films Troma is known for, the studio gets widespread and kind treatment from the press and media. I always attributed this to being authentic and realistic, traits the media greatly appreciated in an industry where far too many believed that their proverbial "shit" did not stink. Troma, on the other hand, had no qualms about their scent, because their arguably stinky films made sense to their fans, and made enough cents to keep the dream alive for over forty years.

The Lesson: Be real. Be authentic. Take your business seriously, but don't take yourself too seriously. Be self-aware about your business, and its role in your industry and the world. Some folks are out there saving lives and curing cancer. Most of us are not, so be true to the true value of your products and services. That's not to diminish them, but rather to present them in the right light and context.

Chapter 26

● ● ●

YES, WE CANNES

2017 marks the seventieth anniversary of the Cannes International Film Festival. This means Troma has been around for more than half of the illustrious festival's existence. What most filmgoers don't realize is that behind the glitz and glamor of the stars and awards, the juries and red carpets, the yachts and parties, there is a vibrant film market going on along the Promenade de la Croisette. Behind the closed doors of suites at the Carlton, the Martinez, and countless other locations along the lovely French Mediterranean backdrop are hundreds of hustlers hawking their films to buyers from all over the globe. Hollywood goes to Cannes to celebrate, Tromaville goes to Cannes to sell!

There are so many stories I have and lessons learned from Cannes that it could be a separate book in its own right. The only time I have ever been in a fist fight in my life was in Cannes, where I was ultimately banned from a restaurant I'd been frequenting for years (starting in my Satori days). A simple, poorly placed Toxie sticker caused a chair-throwing, table-tumbling, all-out brawl. But I digress. I'll tell you the Toxie sticker story another time.

Attending the Cannes Film Market (not the Festival) is intense hard work, made even harder by the realization you are indoors, pitching your celluloid dreams, while outside you are situated in one of the most beautiful places in the world, surrounded by some of the most famous and wealthy people in the world, and representatives of every and any company that means anything in the entertainment world. It is truly heady stuff, and then there you are, hondling over the minimum guarantee for theatrical rights to *Big Gus, What's the Fuss?* in Indonesia. That's show business!

Attending the Cannes Film Festival each year was a very costly endeavor for the Troma Team. Flying four or more Tromites to France was just part of it. Hotels, food, an office suite at one of the main hotels such as the Carlton, all added up to a huge expense for a small, self-made and self-financed entity. We're talking tens of thousands of dollars for a two-week stay, and while the goal is sales, oftentimes the hard results that could be specifically attributed to our attendance at Cannes were quite elusive.

Until one year.

We were set up at the Carlton Hotel, the most expensive, but also most impressive and convenient, place for one to hold court during Cannes. It helped that nobody really understood Troma's business and all were dazzled simply to see this lowly, low-budget outfit offering their wares in the Carlton, alongside the "real" players in international film sales. Of course, in Cannes showmanship is king, and just about anything goes, so it was a perfect venue for the Troma style of guerrilla marketing. Every morning before dawn we blanketed every car parked along the Croisette with flyers for the latest Troma releases. During the day, scantily clad actresses (Tromettes) and costumed creatures (Toxie, Kabukiman, and more) would stroll along the French Riviera along with the Hollywood stars, posing for the press and paparazzi and generally causing a ruckus.

We put on a great show and fought tooth and nail for every foreign market advance we could get—typically we were thrilled to get our hands on checks ranging from $500 to a few thousand bucks, praying they would actually be good when we deposited them back in New York. One year a quiet man, conservatively dressed in a tailored summer suit, came wandering into the Troma suite at the Carlton. We assumed he was lost and looking for some other company. He looked far too normal to have intentionally sought out the Troma team. He soon made it clear that indeed he was in the right place.

"I would like to buy a large package of Troma movies for my territory," he stated.

"What's large?" we wondered.

He went on to put together one of the biggest deals, hundreds of thousands of dollars, that we had ever made in a single sitting. A seriously big deal for the likes of Troma. And we didn't have to sell him. He knew what he wanted, and he wanted it all.

After the agreement was prepared and signed on the spot, and a deposit check was paid, and Lloyd had picked up his jaw from the floor, we asked the gentleman why he was spending so much money on Troma movies? With barely a pause he replied.

"I have been coming to the Cannes Festival for years, and every year I see you guys working it hard and promoting your films. You are always back, reliably, year after year. I have always admired how you promote your brand, but I was never ready to buy any Troma movies for my territory. Now I am ready. I know you are real, and I know you will support your films, because I see you here, doing it year after year."

We shook hands with our new friend and customer, and it was the start of a long and fruitful relationship. It was also a lesson about trade shows and conferences that I have never forgotten.

The Lesson: In most cases, it is very hard to see direct results from attending a trade show or conference that covers the cost of being at the event. On the other hand, if you return to a show, year after year, there is a residual value to being there that doesn't go unnoticed by your customers. If you can be patient, that residual value can pay off years later, and big enough to make all the earlier "dry" years worthwhile. Yes, you Cannes!

Chapter 27

● ● ●

PUTTING OUT FIRES (LITERALLY)

I've never been one to be particularly star struck, mostly because at Satori, in my early twenties, I encountered celebrities on a regular basis as a production assistant and then producer of the Cable TV show *Celebrity*. It didn't take long for me to realize that, regardless of their fortune or fame, celebrities were people too. And like any cross-section of the populace, some celebrities were warm and friendly, and some were complete and utter assholes. Most were in-between, just like you and I, having good and bad moods, good and bad days, and generally behaving within the realm of normalcy.

This proved to be good training for me for throughout my career. At Troma and beyond, I've had the opportunity to work closely with a wide range of high-profile celebrities from William Shatner (while I was in the video-game business) to Akon (while I was in the music-ringtone business) to 50 Cent (in the. CLUB domain-name business). While certainly many celebrities do like to have their ego stroked and appreciate your acknowledging and admiring their work, most of them actually just want to be treated like a regular person and talk with you about regular, mundane, routine stuff.

Except for the assholes. They want to treat you like you are less than them and only want to hear about themselves. Fortunately, in all my years of encountering famous people, I can count the actual A-holes on less than one hand (though a couple of them were pretty bad).

Should you ever have the opportunity to work with celebrities, directly or indirectly, perhaps as spokesperson or endorser of your company or product, remember that while they want to be treated as "talent," they also want to be treated as a person and not an object.

Troma was interesting because while we didn't have many big celebrities in our movies (at least they weren't yet celebrities when they made their Troma debuts), we did have a lot of famous celebrities hang out with us and visit us. Given Troma's raw and fiercely independent stature in (or perhaps more technically, outside of) the entertainment industry, many stars were "friends of Troma" even if they wouldn't be caught dead (or playing dead) in one of our films. Some were friends of Lloyd's going back to his pre-Troma and early Troma days, like Oliver Stone, Roger Corman, Stan Lee, John Voight, Sylvester Stallone, and director John Avildsen (*Rocky*). In the early days, Lloyd worked on films such as *Rocky* and *The Final Countdown* with Kirk Douglas, and made many long-standing friendships through both productions, including a close friendship with Kirk and the Douglas family.

It was not uncommon for some of the abovenamed stars to stop by the Troma building in NY or visit the Troma suite at Cannes or The American Film Market in Los Angeles. This was especially true in the early '90s when *The Toxic Crusaders*, the Saturday-morning cartoon spin-off of *The Toxic Avenger* was momentarily a hot property. During *The Toxic Crusaders'* fifteen minutes of fame, we even had stars like Faye Dunaway coming to see us at AFM. It turned out Dunaway's then nine-year-old son was a big fan of *The Toxic Crusaders*, and she wanted to get her hands on some of the more exclusive Toxic Crusaders toys and products. She even expressed interest in appearing in the Toxic Crusaders movie we were then negotiating with a major studio. Alas, our fifteen minutes expired before we were able to conclude the "big budget" version of *The Toxic Crusaders*.

As I said, I was not particularly star struck in those days, but there was one fairly regular visitor to our American Film Market suite that I was always excited to see, and that was Sam Arkoff. Samuel Z. Arkoff was a true legend in the industry and considered by many to be the god-father of B-movies. In fact, in a memorial he wrote after Sam's death in 2001, famed film critic Roger Ebert called Sam, "the godfather of the beach party and teenage werewolf movies." According to Ebert, "It was said that Sam Arkoff produced more films by Hollywood's best direc-tors and brightest stars than anyone else—and did it the hard way, *before* they were the best or the brightest. AIP films were directed by Francis Ford Coppola, Martin Scorsese, Brian de Palma, and Peter Bogdanovich, and featured early performances by such unknowns as Jack Nicholson, Robert De Niro, Charles Bronson, Barbara Hershey, Nick Nolte, and Peter Fonda—as well as making teen immortals out of Frankie Avalon and Annette Funicello." One of Arkoff's most prolific directors and partners was Roger Corman, who is also credited with giving dozens of Hollywood's finest their start, including James Cameron and producer Gale Ann Hurd (*The Terminator*, TV's *The Walking Dead*).

So, clearly Sam and Lloyd were kindred spirits and got along great, and Sam genuinely admired Lloyd and Troma. When he visited us, he always had great stories to share, and, in true Hollywood mogul style, he always had his signature cigar in hand and mouth. One year Sam stopped by our suite at the American Film Market. I was manning the office myself at the time and had a handful of foreign buyers I was pitching to. Sam said hello and asked if he could just sit and rest for a while. He was in his seventies at the time and wanted to get away from all the commotion in the busy market's hallways and rest a few minutes.

"Of course, Sam, you are always welcome in Tromaville. Make your-self at home!"

And he did. This was back in the day when you could still smoke indoors. Sam plopped down on our couch, grunted a sigh of relief and proceeded to light up his big, fat stogie. I went back to pitching our movies to the other visitors in the suite. After a few minutes, I smelled something burning and turned around to find Sam, sound asleep, snoring peacefully, cigar in mouth, while a big burning ash from his cigar had fallen onto his lapel and was now burning a smoldering hole in his expensive designer suit.

"Sam!" I cried out. "Mr. Arkoff!"

He snored.

His lapel was smoking.

I went over, and, trying not to disturb the lazing legend I brushed the burning ash off his now burnt lapel, and took the still-lit cigar gently from the mouth of the somnolent studio head. Arkoff awoke with a start, grabbed his cigar from me and placed it back in its home between his teeth, closed his eyes, and resumed his nap. Fire hazard avoided, I went back to my startled, and now truly Tromatized buyers.

Yes, in business you always need to be prepared to put out fires. Literally and figuratively.

Chapter 28

● ● ●

SLEEPING ON THE JOB

By the time I joined the Troma Team, I already had a long history with the American Film Market. Satori had been one of the "founding members" when the AMFA (American Film Marketing Association) was formed in 1981, and I had attended every AFM from its inception before I started attending on behalf of Troma. As the name implies, the American Film Market is an annual conference in Los Angeles, where mostly independent film producers and distributors from all over the world gathered to hawk their celluloid wares and find distribution and dollars from territories around the globe.

Given its LA locale, the early days of the AFM were glitzy and glamorous and attracted foreign film buyers (as well as buyers of foreign films) who wanted to get a firsthand taste of Hollywood. The event would be held at hotels such as the Century Plaza back when it truly was one of the premiere hotels in town. There were parties, and celebrities and red carpets, and...Troma!

A section of the hotel served as the market offices. For several floors, the beds had been removed from the hotel rooms so they could serve as offices for each participating seller to hold meetings and pitch their movies. The bedless suites were loaded with VCR machines and TVs to screen films, and their walls were lined with posters and displays for the movies being offered. The buyers would walk up and down the hallways, going in and out of the temporary offices to see what films they might be interested in licensing for distribution.

Troma had one of the offices (which, as noted in the previous chapter, was almost set aflame by a mogul's cigar.) There were strict rules at AFM and the "office suites" had to be empty by a certain time each night, and the office floors were closed until the next day. The proper guest rooms in the Century Plaza were expensive and, being Troma, we couldn't afford to put up everyone in such fine digs. That said, I didn't want to schlepp back and forth through LA traffic each day to stay at a cheap hotel. I volunteered to sleep in the bedless office room (even though it was expressly against the rules).

So, the first night I snuck back onto the office floors and made my way to our suite, and went to bed on the couch, fully dressed, just in case. In the middle of the night, the door to the room opened. It was security.

"Sir? You're not supposed to be here."

Me, startled but thinking fast. "Oh my, I must have fallen asleep! I came back here after dinner to get something I forgot, and I must have fallen asleep. So sorry. Just give me a few minutes, and I'll be on my way."

"Ok. But I'll be checking back in a few minutes, so you need to leave this floor."

"Yes, sir. Of course, sir..."

Alone again, I pondered my predicament. I had nowhere to go, and it was almost 3:00 a.m. Then the proverbial light bulb went off above my head. The wall behind the couch had floor-to-ceiling poster displays we had put up to decorate the suite and turn it into a mini Tromaville displaying our movies. I pulled the couch away a few inches and then pulled the poster displays up against the back of the couch. This created a gap between the posters and the wall that was just wide enough for me to slide behind. And slide behind I did. Lying on the floor behind the posters, invisible, I waited. Sure enough, soon the door to the room opened and I could hear the security guard step into the room and turn on the light to see that I was no longer there (as far as he could tell). He shut the lights and left. I held my breath a moment or two longer, and then exhaled with relief and fell asleep. The next morning, I made sure I was up early and showered and changed and out the door for breakfast long before the morning cleaning crew would come through.

And that's how it went, every night. I'd sneak back into the room and squeeze into my little cave behind the poster displays and hope and pray I wasn't snoring when the security guard made his rounds in the middle of the night. And you thought the movie industry was glamorous! Hey, if George Costanza can sleep under his desk I can certainly catch some zzzs hiding behind the couch in a bedless hotel suite. It's all good.

The truth is, when you're a start-up and operating on limited resources, you have to get creative and be willing to do things "the big guys" might not consider. For me, aside from adding a bit of intrigue and adventure to my trip, sleeping surreptitiously in the suite saved the company money and me time. I was happy to be taking one for the Troma Team.

Would you make a similar sacrifice for your team? Have you ever put up with unusual conditions just to get the job done?

Chapter 29

● ● ●

RAISING YOUR HAND

In business, there are many theories about doing things "in-house" versus "outsourcing" or hiring agencies, consultants, so-called experts, and other third parties to work on your company's behalf. It is a decision entrepreneurs struggle with all the time, and in truth, the decision is based on much more than a cost-benefit analysis. There are other considerations, including your company culture, to think about when deciding what roles your employees play versus the roles of outsiders.

In Tromaville this decision was easier to make, as we didn't have the resources (or mind-set, for that matter) to hire someone from outside to do the work someone inside could do cheaper (and, perhaps better, but mainly cheaper). After all, when we were in production, we were known for throwing inexperienced people into uncharted waters and hoping for the best. Why wouldn't the same philosophy apply when we operated the business side of things? For the most part, it did.

When we were growing and making more deals, our legal bills were growing as well, as we had to run everything by "outside counsel." Instead of continuing to pay the pros exorbitant fees, we hired a young, green law school graduate who had probably spent far more time in a bar than studying for and passing the Bar. He was eager to work, had no practical experience yet, and thus was willing to work for very little in order to gain real-world experience as "in-house" counsel for an established independent movie studio. (It sounds good on paper, doesn't it?)

In truth, David G was a bright, eager, somewhat conservative addition to the Troma Team. (You will note that in previous chapters I use people's actual names; however, in this case I have chosen to say "David G" instead of our lawyer's real name. I ain't stupid. He is a lawyer, after all…). In truth, as with many who passed through Tromaville and passed their sink-or-swim test, David proved to be a genuinely talented attorney who may have learned by fire at Troma, but also earned the respect of an industry and went on to have a great career as a leading entertainment attorney.

Having a young, in-house attorney is something I learned from Troma that I have lobbied for at every company I have worked at since, and I have always hired one at every company I have founded and have been in control of. Sure, you still will need the expertise of out-house counsel from time to time, but having someone on your payroll to do as much of the legal legwork as possible, and then letting the high-priced pros review it, will pay for itself in no time. Plus, an in-house legal beagle will truly and fully understand the ins and outs of your business in ways "the big guys" never will, and your inside guy or gal will create a sense of checks and balances with the outside firm of record. It may seem frivolous for a small start-up of ten or twelve employees to have an attorney on staff, but I can assure you from experience it can be a tremendous benefit and cost savings in the long run.

Clearly, in Tromaville the culture was one of DIY at every possible turn, which is how I suddenly found myself at the heart of the licensing and merchandising industry. We were in the midst of launching *The Toxic Crusaders*, the cartoon spin-off of *The Toxic Avenger* that was going to be produced as a Saturday-morning cartoon series, made by the same animation studio, MWS, that had been responsible for the megasuccessful animated *TMNT: Teenage Mutant Ninja Turtles*. The Turtles had emerged from the shell of a popular underground comic to become one of the biggest TV, toy and game phenomenon in history. Kids everywhere were obsessed with the adventures of Michelangelo, Donatello, Leonardo, and

Raphael, and a gazillion dollars were being spent on *TMNT* toys, games, clothes, and anything capable of having a logo printed on it. The *Teenage Mutant Ninja Turtles* were an industry, and at that moment it appeared that *The Toxic Crusaders* were ideally positioned to be next in line for the kids' cartoon and merchandising throne.

Miraculously, Toxie was loved by the industry that had made the Turtles massive. Like the *TMNT*, Toxie was edgy, action-packed, and had an underlying positive message—pro-environment and anti–toxic waste. (Toxie knew firsthand the perils of that!) We were shell-shocked by the attention but managed to line up the animation deal with MWS (same as *TMNT*) and a master toy license with Playmates Toys (same as *TMNT*). We had the "A" team behind us and woke up every day pinching ourselves to test the realization that kids everywhere would soon be looking up to a hideously deformed creature of superhuman size and strength that first gained notoriety in a trashy, uber-violent, R-rated, low-budget, low-brow cult movie. The irony was not lost on anyone. The engine of greed salivating for the next *TMNT* made it all OK.

So as the animated series commenced production and the Playmates toy line began taking its hideously deformed shape (in the form of neon-green Toxie action figures and accessories) we were suddenly the darlings of an industry we knew nothing about. Suddenly we were being courted by every major licensing agent in the industry, from Surge Licensing, the team behind the *TMNT* merchandising machine generating hundreds of millions of dollars in royalties, to a literal parade of agencies and agents ascending our narrow stairs to enter Tromaville and trying to convince us to sign over our exclusive rights for them to represent.

One guy literally showed up with a check for $50,000 that he insisted we take as a deposit against the millions of dollars of royalty fees he would soon be raining upon us. We didn't have an agreement or contract with him. He just handed us a check. Lloyd held it, briefly, until Michael promptly swiped it from him, and inspected it carefully. $50,000 was a lot of dough in Tromaville in those days. We made entire movies for $50,000. And this guy was ready to hand it over to us, over a property he barely knew anything about. I suppose Gordon Gekko was right: "Greed is good." Thanks to the Teenage Mutant Ninja Turtles, when people in the licensing industry looked at Toxie, they did not see his grossly wrinkled skin or droopily deformed eye. All they saw was green. And not the green of his toxically tanned skin, but rather the green of money.

The whole thing made us, the proud purveyors of so-called schlock, feel a bit "icky."

After the wave of eager agents had subsided and we were able to reflect on our newfound role as the apparent object of everyone's affection, we realized that all of our suitors had one thing in common. They all wanted to keep one-third of all the money we would make from *The Toxic Crusaders*. That seemed to be the industry standard. They'd go out and make licensing deals with the manufacturers of sneakers and bedsheets and pajamas and school supplies and underwear and coloring books and anything and everything else they could, and in return, they'd keep a full 33.33 percent of what we collected from such deals. From where we sat that was a pretty steep commission.

So I raised my hand.

"How hard can this be?" I asked Lloyd and Michael. "I mean, it's not rocket science, and we already have all the manufacturers interested in *The Toxic Crusaders* thanks to the TV series and Playmates Toys. Why should we give up a third? I'll do it."

And with that, Troma Licensing was formed, and I was it.

It was dive in head first and sink or swim. I was, fortunately, able to swim and soon became entrenched in the world of licensing and merchandising. In truth, it is an amazing industry, at the time led by many sincere and hardworking manufacturers that were often long-standing family businesses, like Wormser Pajamas. As a kid, I wore Batman pajamas made by Wormser, so it was truly a thrill to get to know and work with Ed Wormser and his team to make Toxic Crusaders PJs. And it seemed everyone in the close-knit industry was warm, friendly, and eager to see Toxie succeed.

I was very glad I raised my hand.

When new opportunities arise for your business, before you hire the so-called experts, could you create an expert from within?

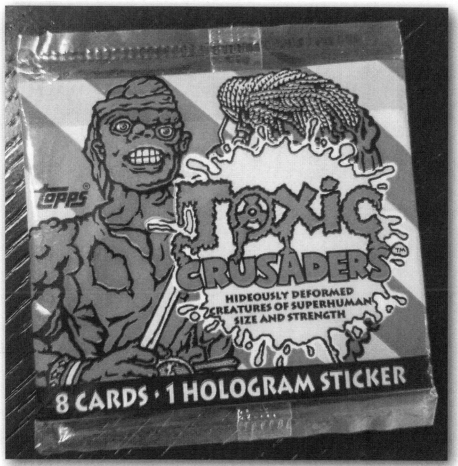

An unopened pack of Topps *Toxic Crusaders* trading cards
(From the author's personal collection)

Chapter 30

● ● ●

IN WHAT UNIVERSE COULD *THE TOXIC AVENGER* AND *READING RAINBOW* COEXIST? THE TROMA UNIVERSE

Despite our naiveté, or perhaps because of it (but mostly because of the support of MWS and Playmates to drive the belief that *The Toxic Crusaders* would become the next *Teenage Mutant Ninja Turtles*), we enjoyed a fair amount of early success making licensing deals for Toxie. In fact, by the time the animated TV series was on the air, we had done more than seventy deals with manufacturers around the world for every imaginable product, from the obvious comic books (Marvel) and computer games (Sega and Nintendo), to T-shirts, pajamas, school supplies, sneakers, stickers, trading cards, coloring books, bed sheets and blankets, and on and on and on. They were fun and exciting times, and we were literally the life of the party. (Did I mention we also made a deal for *Toxic Crusaders* party supplies? We did.)

Once we were so deeply entrenched in the licensing world, we realized that representing more properties than just Toxie would be easier now that we already had the manufacturer contacts. We were regularly meeting with these folks and were building solid friendships and business relationships. Representing other properties in addition to *The Toxic Crusaders* would not actually require us to add any staff or do anything differently; we could just have more products to sell to the people we were already selling Toxie to. Like I said when I first raised my hand, this was not rocket science.

As far as our own properties went, there weren't many that potentially lent themselves to the licensing world. Would someone want *Surf Nazis must Die* or *Rabid Grannies* pajamas? We were in the early stages of planning for *Sgt. Kabukiman NYPD*, and we recognized the potential in that super-hero storyline to appeal to kids, so we decided to steer it more toward a PG-13 direction and potentially seek animation and licensing deals for *Kabukiman* (and eventually, a pretty good animated pilot was done by a leading animator, DIC Entertainment). But *Kabukiman* wasn't yet ready for prime time, and the rest of the Troma catalog was slime pickens, er slim pickings, from a licensing perspective, so once again I raised my hand.

"We could look for other properties we could represent for licensing and merchandising!"

Lloyd and Michael agreed, and so we did.

Reading Rainbow was an Emmy Award-winning PBS series starring Levar Burton. The acclaimed educational show was a coproduction of the Public Broadcasting Stations out of Buffalo New York and Lincoln Nebraska, but the actual production was done by a New York-based company, Lancit Productions. I had some contacts at Lancit, and after doing some research and realizing that *Reading Rainbow* had not done any licensing or merchan-dising of their well-respected brand, I reached out to the folks I knew at Lancit and got an introduction to the show's executive producer, Twila Liggett, from the Lincoln Nebraska station.

The first time Twila and I spoke, if she had any inkling of the types of films Troma was known for, she didn't let on. I wasn't hiding anything, of course, but I focused my pitch on the success we had had thus far with *The Toxic Crusaders*, and the positive environmental message the characters stood for. I touted our strong relations with manufacturers and explained how a popular show like *Reading Rainbow* could generate additional revenue and exposure by licensing products such as books, games, and T-shirts to utilize the *Reading Rainbow* brand. Twila was intrigued. Because the show focused on introducing children to existing books, there were really no characters, per se, that a licensing property would typically have, and for that reason, they never really thought to pursue any licensing deals. How could we do differently?

I had an idea, which I explained to Twila. We could develop some artwork around the *Reading Rainbow* theme, and incorporate the widely-recognized *Reading Rainbow* logo into the art, and license that artwork to manufacturers. We could also seek other deals where new products can be created under the *Reading Rainbow* theme, without having to utilize *Reading Rainbow* show content. Twila was skeptical but interested enough to invite me to come to Washington, DC, when she was going to be there with her Buffalo PBS partner so that I could pitch them both. So, I had our poster artist create some artwork based on the idea that "reading is king" with a classic "king" character and a bunch of multiethnic kids. I had him draw some samples of the art on some different products, and off to Washington I went.

I met the PBS folks in a Washington hotel room, spread out my art samples on the hotel bed and pitched my heart out. I acknowledged the challenge *Reading Rainbow* presented but stood firm that if any company could stand up to the challenge, Troma could. After all, we had taken a crass, R-Rated character and turned him into a kid-friendly cartoon, with a positive environmental message. Miraculously, they bought into the belief, and we were able to make a deal. Troma Licensing was now representing the Emmy Award-winning PBS TV show, *Reading Rainbow*. And there was not a single ice cube in hell.

While not a blockbuster, we were able to successfully make a handful of deals on behalf of *Reading Rainbow*, including a high-profile deal for a series of educational CD-ROM games with GameTek, then one of the leaders in the Sega and Nintendo cartridge game world, looking to break into the newly emerging CD-ROM platform. After the successful addition of *Reading Rainbow* to the Troma Licensing catalog, we were eager to seek out other properties to represent and eventually also made some deals on behalf of *The Cat Hall of Fame* and the classic Japanese cartoon, *Gigantor* (and the relationship we established with GameTek eventually led to my departure from Tromaville to go work for them).

There were many great lessons in the Troma Licensing experience, and I still relish in the fact we were able to convince an award-winning PBS children's show to come under the same roof as *The Toxic Avenger*. I credit that victory to passion and creativity, and the Troma culture of authenticity. We turned the potential liability of Toxie into an asset that demonstrated the depth of our abilities. We were passionate about Toxie and could bring that passion to our approach to their show, and we had an outlook that was different, and that showed in our ideas of creative ways to make licensing work for a property that, while acclaimed and successful, didn't necessarily fit the traditional model for licensing success.

Don't be afraid to pursue an opportunity because it seems impossible (as Troma and PBS working together most certainly seemed at first). In business, passion and creativity can and do overcome what might seem to be the more logical path. If you believe in it, go for it. What was our risk? The cost of some artwork mock-ups and a trip to Washington, DC (and perhaps the potential embarrassment of a decided "no"). Certainly worth it.

Chapter 31

● ● ●

GIVE CREDITS WHERE CREDIT IS DUE

A re you the type of person who watches and reads all the credits at the end of a movie or TV show? It's OK, you can admit it. I do too. The credits at the end of a film or TV show are mesmerizing for some, as we look through the regular sounding names of regular people and realize they've had the irregular opportunity to participate in that glamorous experience of making a movie. Watching credits is also where we learned, for the very first time, about positions such as "key grip" and "best boy." If you are one so fortunate to be listed in the credits, they are the proof of the pudding that you were involved in the making of the film. Regardless of how large or small your role may have been, it is an exciting moment to see your name up on the silver screen. This is a universal truth. *Everybody* gets a thrill seeing their name in the credits of a film or TV project.

The people surrounding a Troma production are no different, and understanding the power of that universal truth, Troma is extremely generous with who gets listed in the end-credits of a Troma film. And why not? It literally costs the production nothing to add some names to the end-credits, and if you can use that gift as a currency or just as a simple acknowledgment of someone's official or unofficial contribution to the cause, why not? They'll be forever grateful, and I do mean forever because the credits of a movie are truly a lasting tribute.

When we produced *Sgt. Kabukiman NYPD*, my son Zach was eighteen months old. I brought him along with me to the set once when we were filming on a weekend in Prospect Park, Brooklyn. The director (Lloyd) offered to put Zach in a scene, and sure enough in the midst of an action scene in the park, there's a cutaway to a reaction shot of a group of bystanders watching the action. That illustrious group of extras, er, background actors, included Lloyd's dad, the late, truly great, Stanley Kaufman, and my son Zachary in the arms of a large, mean-looking thug (just my young son was in the arms of the thug, not Lloyd's dad). Today Zach has a son of his own, older than Zach was for his on-screen debut, and to this day adult Zach shows off his name in the credits of *Kabukiman* and the associated IMDB listing. It is a badge of honor he is proud to display.

So, the next time you watch a Troma film, stick around for the end credits. In addition to quite a few not-so-hidden puns and jokes, you might also find the names of lawyers, accountants, cousins, pets, pizza delivery persons, and anyone and everyone who might have directly or indirectly touched the production, even if just for a moment. Credits, even where credit might not actually be due, but as a small token of appreciation that is valued by the recipient far greater than its actual cost to the production.

The Lesson: When you think about it, isn't that what recognition is all about? What does it cost you to acknowledge a job well done? Nothing. Yet to the person on the receiving end of that recognition it may mean a great deal. And you don't have to be the boss to offer recognition. One of the most powerful ways to gain respect and admiration is to be the one who recognizes their peers and acknowledges their accomplishments both privately to them, and when appropriate, publicly. In Tromaville, where I was surrounded by folks desperately trying to find their way and do the right thing without much experience or guidance, I learned the power of giving credit and praise when someone did well.

This is not just a fact of Tromaville, though that's where the lesson hit home for me, and I've tried to be generous and aware of giving praise and recognition ever since. The truth is that numerous studies have shown that when it comes to employee motivation, recognition is often a better impetus than more money. Are you giving credit where credit is due? How can you better leverage giving credit? And by the way, this is not just a good business practice. Giving recognition works with children if you are a parent, and with your partner, if you are in a relationship. Don't you like receiving praise? Of course, you do. So does everyone else in your world; so be the giver as often as you can. It may not have the permanence of a film credit, but the credit you give will have an impact, and a positive one.

My son Zach with his trusty pacifier, and Lloyd's dad, Stanley (Screen capture from *Sgt. Kabukiman NYPD*)

Chapter 32

● ● ●

THE STALKING DEAD

One needed to stoop no lower than the stoops of the steps of the Troma Building to find the next gaggle of gore, and at the time, one of the very first "shot-on-video" productions to gain "professional" distribution on VHS. Yes, I am referring to the aptly titled, hillbilly horror extravaganza, *Redneck Zombies.*

To beat the traffic into Manhattan from my humble abode in Rockland County, I started my commute early, and I would often be the first to arrive at the office, giving me the honor of unlocking and sliding open the rolling steel gate that completely covered the entry way to the Troma building. On one particularly brisk morning, I stepped over two well-bundled-up young lads huddled together on the single stoop beneath the steel-enclosed entrance. I assumed they were members of the neighborhood homeless (this was Hell's Kitchen, after all) and so I did my best not to disturb them as I removed the bulky Masterlock and rolled the gate up into its well.

Well, they did awaken and gazed up at me through glassy red eyes and gruff, unshaven faces. They looked the part but seemed a bit young to be homeless already. One of them, the chubbier of the two, coughed, smiled and spoke softly to me.

"Is this the Troma Building?"

"It is," I replied, surprised that such street urchins would actually know where they are.

"Cool," he muttered back at me, and elbowed his companion, "This is it!"

Duty called, and I also had to get to work, so I reattached the lock in its resting place, opened the door and headed upstairs to my desk. As the rest of the Troma Team arrived over the next hours, a few folks mentioned the "two dudes" sitting outside the front door. Surprised that they were still hanging around now that the day was underway, I went back downstairs to confront them.

"Hey guys, this is a business. You can't just sit here all day."

"We know it's a business. It's Troma!" the bigger guy exclaimed. He seemed to have woken up a bit since our last encounter, and there was a certain spark in his eye. "We came all the way from Maryland to meet Lloyd Kaufman, and we slept here all night, right, Ed?" He was invoking his shivering associate, who just grunted.

Needless to say, I was surprised to find out that these seemingly bumbling bums were actually camped out in our dirty doorway intentionally.

"Um," I muttered. "Do you have an appointment?"

"No, dude. We didn't have a number to call, so we just took the bus down from Maryland and walked here from Port Authority."

Of course, it was the more rotund dude doing the talking. His cohort "Ed" was clearly the quiet type. The pair's spokesperson continued.

"We came all the way here to show *this* to Lloyd!"

And he reached into his knapsack to pull out a couple of well-worn plastic 3/4" U-Matic videotapes.

"It's our film, dude. We made it. Shot entirely on video, a full-length feature film, totally inspired by Lloyd and Troma. We love Troma! We're huge Troma fans. Do you work for Troma?"

"I do. That's why I stepped over you to open the office this morning. I work here, and I've got to get back to work now." And I turned to head back up the stairs.

"Dude…" The pleading in his voice stopped me. He continued.

"Dude, so, can we see him? Can we meet Lloyd? It'll only take a minute. We just want to shake his hand, tell him how much he means to us, and

100

give him our film. He's gotta see it. We made it for him. We made it because of him, because of Troma."

Behind the wind-burnt rosy cheeks, beneath the unshaven, unkempt face, there was a genuine sincerity in the kid's demeanor that touched me. The other kid, Ed, the silent one, he might as well have been a zombie, just gawking at us lifelessly. Little did I know.

"I'm Pericles, Peri. Peri Lewnes, and this is my partner, Ed. Ed Bishop. We came all the way here from Mary..."

"I know, I know, you came all the way from Maryland, and you slept here all night. Did you really sleep here all night?"

I only had to look at them for the answer. They had definitely spent the night sleeping on the cold stone stoop at the gateway to Tromaville.

"Let me see what I can do. Wait here."

And we all chuckled at the irony of my statement. Waiting was all they could do and all they had done. Even Ed smiled.

Back upstairs I waited for there to be a brief pause in the yelling and screaming coming from behind the closed door to Lloyd and Michael's office. I knocked and then opened the door enough to stick my head in to see the pages of what once must have been a screenplay strewn about the office, typed papers scattered across the floor, and on both of the mogul's desks. They had just completed a productive, creative meeting.

"What is it, Sass?" Lloyd bellowed.

"Um, did you notice two guys sitting on the stoop when you came in this morning?"

"The homeless guys? They were asleep, so I let them be."

"Yeah, well, they're not homeless, they're stalkers. Well, I mean fans. They've been hanging out all night and want to meet with you."

"Fuck that," grumped Lloyd.

"OK, should I tell them to leave? They made a film they want to show you. Shot it on video."

"What's it called?"

"I didn't ask."

"Well, have them come up and sit."

"You'll meet with them?"

"No, but let them get out of the cold and warm up inside Tromaville... and find out what the name of their film is!"

So I invited Peri and Ed to enter Tromaville and come up the stairs and sit in the two mismatched chairs against the wall beside the so-called reception desk.

"Can we meet with Lloyd?" Peri perked up from his new indoor perch.

"I don't know. Hey, what's your film called anyway?" Peri smiled, genuinely proud.

"*Redneck Zombies*! It's truly disgusting, and funny too. I did all the effects myself. Ed's my producing partner. There's some seriously gross shit in it. Lloyd will love it."

Several hours later the producing pair from Maryland were still sitting quietly in their chairs. They truly didn't seem to mind, happy to be in from the cold and able to get whatever small sniff of the Eau du Troma they could from their front-row seats in the corner of the office. Lloyd came out of his office a few times and walked by them, paying them little notice. They were thrilled nonetheless. At some point, I did tell Lloyd the clever title of their film. We both agreed it was a good title.

Finally, sometime in the late afternoon, Lloyd invited the two patient and persistent purveyors of a perverse film into the inner sanctum. We all gathered in the center of Lloyd and Michael's office, dragging in some extra chairs to accommodate the unscheduled crowd.

"Let's see it!" Lloyd dived in, bypassing the usual niceties. "Your movie, let's see it! I hope it's as good as the title. Something *Zombies*, right?"

"*Redneck Zombies*," Peri stated proudly as he withdrew the tapes from his pack. Lloyd popped one of the tapes into the machine connected to a 19" TV on top of a tall metal filing cabinet. The cathode ray tube popped to life with a close-up of human intestines being chomped on by an over-weight zombie in a flannel shirt, overalls, and a red trucker hat. The fact that it was shot on video and not film gave the gore a certain je ne sais quoi that Lloyd found quite appealing.

"This is great," he commented.

Peri and Ed beamed.

And from that humble beginning began a great business collaboration. The patience of the boys from Maryland paid off, and their dream of having their feisty little film distributed by Troma came true. We made a deal to take on *Redneck Zombies* in all its visceral video glory, despite the many challenges a shot-on-video production would create (it was essentially considered "undistributable" at first). Even for a schlocky horror flick, the value for a meaningful home-video release was created by a small theatrical release, and back then the technology for video to film transfers was still crude and expensive. Yet there was something strangely appealing about Ed and Peri's movie. And *Redneck Zombies* was a great, marketable title, right up there with *Rabid Grannies*. So, with a nervous, sweaty handshake and a modest advance guarantee, *Redneck Zombies* became the latest addition to the growing Troma film library.

Mission accomplished, Ed quietly took the next bus back to Maryland. Peri, on the other hand, had become quite comfortable living on our front stoop and decided to stay. He continued to stalk us—er, hang out around Tromaville—until finally, Lloyd offered him a job as we geared up for *Troma's War*.

Peri is an extremely talented and hardworking filmmaker and went on to handle a wide range of duties in *Troma's War*, *Toxic Avenger II* and *III*, and *Sgt. Kabukiman NYPD*. Peri served us well in front of and behind the cameras as an actor, stunt person, effects artist, second-unit director, cameraperson and, on at least one occasion, hired heavy—knocking out an unruly production assistant with a single well-placed punch. There wasn't anything Peri wasn't willing to do for the cause of making a film. Remember the close-up of a mouthful of live worms at the beginning of *Kabukiman*? That's Peri's mouth. And just letting the vermin squirm around in his cheeks wasn't enough for Peri. He had to chew and swallow a few for authenticity. Pericles Lewnes is the real deal.

The Lesson: I learned a lot from Peri and the *Redneck Zombies* story. Persistence and patience are often the key to the payoff. And you have to believe in yourself before anyone else will believe in you. Peri and Ed were believers. They made *Redneck Zombies* with a clear mission in mind. It *would* become a Troma Team release. They never stopped believing that, and they were more than happy to do whatever it took, even sleeping on the cold hard reality of a Hell's Kitchen stoop just to demonstrate their unwavering belief in said mission. Granted, things don't always work out the way you want just because you believe, but your chances are certainly better if you are truly committed to your cause.

There's also a lesson in Lloyd's willingness to see talent and good in something regardless of the wrapper it shows up in. At the time we acquired *Redneck Zombies,* there was literally no such thing as a film shot only on video getting any sort of mainstream distribution. Peri and Ed's little film was the first. Lloyd knew it was good and deserved to be seen (especially by Troma fans) so he was willing to give it a shot when others would have said no solely on the fact that it was not shot on film. But good is good, and Troma knows its audience. *Redneck Zombies* has enjoyed continued success as a Troma classic ever since, and today nobody thinks twice about a "film" shot entirely on video. It is OK to be the first. Just because something has not been done before doesn't mean it can't break through and be successful. If Lloyd and Troma had stuck to the conventional wisdom of the time, we'd never have touched a "film" that was not shot on film, and *Redneck Zombies* may never have found its place in film gore history.

Chapter 33

● ● ●

TACKLING NON-TOXIC TECHNOLOGY

When I first arrived in Tromaville, in 1987, it was a land of Luddites. We had phones (landlines), and typewriters (at least they were of the electric sort), and perhaps our greatest bit of hi-tech wonderment was a telex machine. A telex machine enabled you to send and receive short text messages, printed on a roll of paper, to any other telex machine in the world, as long as you had their correct telex address (number). It was a very rudimentary system. You typed in the other party's telex number on a keyboard. When the correct connection was made and confirmed, you typed the rest of the message and pushed "SEND." The receiving telex machine printed out your message at the other end. There were no electronic copies. If the telex printer jammed or if you forgot to load a new roll of paper in the machine, you risked not receiving intended messages.

As Troma's business is and has always been very international (and in fact, at the time the bulk of our measly revenue came from abroad—not a woman, but rather foreign territories that licensed the rights to distribute our films in nether, er, other, regions) deals were often negotiated and consummated through a series of telex messages over several days. Given the international time zone differences, communication by telex was about as asymmetric as you can get. Each day we'd send out a slew of telex messages to various foreign partners and potential partners. In the evening, before shutting down Tromaville for the day, it was someone's responsibility to make sure there was a full roll of paper in the telex machine and that it was on. The following morning, the first thing the first person to arrive in the office would do would be to check the telex machine for the various responses and other incoming messages. Some days the paper roll of incoming telexes could be several feet long. These messages from afar, like smoke signals, were our lifeblood. It was a bad day when there were no incoming telexes on the machine, and a worse day if someone had forgotten to load the paper the night before. Did I ever mention that Lloyd was known to yell on occasion?

You may be wondering why the telex was so important, and why didn't we just call people on the phone. If that's what you are wondering, then you surely grew up in the age of the mobile phone and have no recollection of how complicated (and expensive) international phone calls once were. As a method of conducting international business, phones were actually incredibly unreliable and inefficient. And did I mention that overseas calls were *expensive*? First, you were never guaranteed a good connection. Second, you were never guaranteed that the person you were calling would actually answer the phone, especially given the time differences. Third, there was a good chance the party you were calling didn't speak very well English, making voice-only business negotiations subject to all sorts of misunderstandings and miscommunications. Thus, the slower but written telex was a far more reliable means of conducting business. By definition, every discussion was confirmed in writing and far less likely to be misinterpreted.

While the international film business was heavily reliant on the telex, there was a newfangled new technology starting to gain some steam in the United States. It was called a facsimile machine, and you are probably more familiar with it as a fax machine. Unlike the telex, which required a special dedicated line, a fax machine could connect to a regular phone line, and transmit full documents, even rudimentary black and white images, to any other fax machine, creating a very reasonable facsimile of whatever papers you passed through its scanners. The early fax machines were monsters, big and expensive, the size of a large laser printer and nearly $2,000. We were content with our relatively petite and simple telex machine until Jere Hausfater came along.

Jere (pronounced Jerry), was the in-house lawyer for Media Home Entertainment, the Los Angeles-based home-video giant leading the charge into the VHS market. We were in the midst of negotiating what for Troma would be a very significant multipicture, presell deal, guaranteeing us a substantial midsix figure advance for each of the films in the package. Plus, we'd be getting a high-profile home-video release for each film from one of the top distributors in the business. It was a big deal for us. And Jere, in his infinite wisdom, had decided he would *only* conduct contract negotiations via fax. This was the future, he insisted, and everyone in Hollywood was doing their deals this way, sending contract drafts back and forth over the phone lines. He basically gave us an ultimatum. "If you want this deal to happen, you need to get a fax machine." And so we did, as much as the hefty price tag pained us. The "telex" corner by the bathroom was now getting crowded with technology, and yet another machine with rolls of paper to attend to.

As if getting a fax machine wasn't enough, I was putting increasing pressure on Lloyd and Michael for us to get a computer. The IBM PC had begun to make its mark, and the idea of a personal computer was beginning to take shape on desks at many businesses. I explained how word processing software would make our lives infinitely better than it had been at the mercy of our old typewriters, not to mention being able to run spreadsheets and financial models to help streamline our preproduction processes. The argument worked, and soon Tromaville became computer literate.

Why stop with fax machines and computers? Now that Troma was tech savvy, we decided to go all out and get our hands on one of the very first "mobile" phones. The word mobile is in quotes because these early Motorola specials were hardly the pocketable portables we are accustomed to today. The early cell phone had a thick curly cord, just like the landline phones, and that cord was connected to a cumbersome and awkward battery base unit about the size and weight of three bricks strapped together with a handle. We were getting ready to commence production on *Troma's War*, and Lloyd's wife Pat was pregnant, and due to deliver right about the time we'd be filming in the middle of nowhere, on the deserted beaches of Caumsett State Park on Long Island. So it was decided we'd rent one of these massive mobile phones to keep the production connected to civilization (and mostly to have a means of Pat contacting Lloyd should the momentous moment arrive while he was on set).

As the line producer and resident gadget geek, the mobile phone became my responsibility and my 24-7 companion. Needless to say, my (now-ex) wife didn't love the fact that I lugged that beast with me all weekend long as we ran errands and entertained our young son. But I did. We were in the thick of things with shooting at Caumsett just days away, and now Lloyd could contact me at any time to yell and scream about one crisis or another. The only saving grace was that calls were around $1.25 per minute on that thing, so Lloyd's miser mind kept him from just calling me to chat. He reserved calling me on mobile for the times he truly had something worthy of screaming about. In truth, and as a peek into the future, even the hefty handheld phone was a very useful asset during production, when all sorts of shit were constantly flying through the air and could hit the fan at any moment. Being able to make or receive an important production-related call anytime, anywhere, saved the day on more than one occasion, helping to justify the more than $1,000 per week the darn thing was costing us. I was decidedly sad the day I had to return the rental phone and go back to my primitive, disconnected ways.

But Troma had crossed the line into our technology-driven future, and I found more and more ways to leverage Troma to feed my own gadget geek desires. Now that we had computers, we had access to this up and coming thing called e-mail. Initially, e-mail became popular on the university-run computer systems, and folks with a .edu e-mail address were among the first to adopt the now-ubiquitous communication system. We were dealing with some talented stop-motion filmmakers who had "day jobs" at a Midwestern university. It was our early adoption of e-mail that gave us easy access to the guys and eventually distribution rights to one of their films.

Then came Compuserve. Prior to the explosion of the World Wide Web as we know it today, the "Internet" was generally accessed through two major self-contained subscription-based networks, Prodigy and Compuserve. Compuserve was the first and largest, with around 600,000 subscribers in 1990 and Prodigy, owned by CBS, IBM, and Sears, had around 465,000. Both services operated as Internet Service Providers, offering their customers dial-up access to "the net" along with rudimentary e-mail and other information services. Prodigy was the first to provide a more graphical user interface, while Compuserve featured a menu-driven command line structure. I can still remember having to type "TOP" at the command line to get to the main Compuserve menu. You could think of them both as precursors to the more popular America Online (AOL) which, after experiencing enormous growth thanks to their massive "disk giveaway" marketing programs, ended up acquiring and absorbing Compuserve.

One rarely thinks of Troma as a technology trendsetter, but the truth is, before anyone had ever done anything similar, we actually were conducting "live" online chats with a movie character. This was in 1991– 1992, before the advent of the World Wide Web as we know it today. Compuserve had established many very active "forums" where like-minded users would gather and engage in discussion boards. One of the most popular was the "Showbiz Forum," where I was an active member, both personally and on behalf of Troma. There were truly no similar outlets at the time, and thus the Compuserve Showbiz Forum attracted not only the computer-literate fans of the entertainment industry but also many industry professionals who were also early technology adopters, including the likes of film critic Roger Ebert, who was a frequent forum participant (and a very supportive Troma fan, I might add.)

At one point during the heyday of *The Toxic Crusaders*, we started promoting the chance to "chat live" with Toxie in the Compuserve Showbiz Forum. We'd announce a scheduled time that Toxie would appear in the forum, and at the appointed hour I would log on as Toxie and answer, in real time, any questions forum members would have, allowing them to engage in an actual online conversation with their favorite hideously deformed creature of superhuman size and strength. Today, in the age of Twitter, Facebook, Snapchat, and Instagram, where celebrities and fictional characters can have literally millions of active followers online, having a faux Toxie chat with a dozen or so forum members must sound silly. Trust me when I tell you it was truly groundbreaking at the time (and perhaps a little heartbreaking too, when one considers the Showbiz Forum was probably mostly inhabited by adult male nerds—myself plainly included...). Still, it was cool, and Troma's adoption of new technology has continued to this day, with Troma being one of the first "studios" to distribute full-length feature films on mobile, and with the widespread streaming of Troma films on platforms like YouTube and services such as Troma Now.

The Lesson: Technology is your friend. Don't be afraid to experiment with and adopt new technologies and platforms as they can readily lead to new business models and new distribution channels and audiences for your product or service. In truth, there are few better examples of technology opening new doors than the film-distribution business, and especially for a studio like Troma, which was building an extensive library of content. When I first joined Troma, the primary outlet for its movies was in theaters. Then home video came along, and films that hadn't earned a dime in years suddenly had new life (and value) breathed into them thanks to the VHS industry. Then doors opened on cable and pay TV, and we found ourselves licensing those same movies to USA Network and other TV outlets. Then VHS became DVD, and DVD became streaming, at each juncture creating new opportunities to repurpose content (i.e., films) that were initially created for an entirely different medium.

Yes, technology often leads to disruption, but if you can figure out how to ride the wave of disruption, technology can expand, rather than constrict your business. What new tech trends can you leverage to grow your business? Can VR and AR have an impact on what you do? Mobile? Wearables? Where can you overlay your product or service on the latest new tech? If you can figure that out, you may see new ways to grow your business, just as Troma has evolved alongside tech to grow theirs.

Chapter 34

● ● ●

THE DIRECTOR'S CHAIR AND THE TROMAMERCIAL

Vinnie Favale, back then, was "Vinny from shipping" at the then-nascent cable TV channel Comedy Central. Vinny, an awesome guy, was also a big Troma fan and wanted to make his move over to the programming side of the Comedy Central House. We had a wacky idea to do an actual thirty-minute infomercial that was both a spoof of the then-popular late-night infomercials, and at the same time really was an infomercial selling an actual package of crazy Troma products and memorabilia, put together as "The Troma System." Vinny loved it, and in his infinite skill, vision, and wisdom managed to get his bosses at Comedy Central to agree to broadcast the "Tromamercial."

Today, Vinny is a top programming executive at CBS, who was responsible for the Late Show with David Letterman and its successors, and he's been a frequent guest on the Howard Stern Show. We'd like to think it is thanks to The Troma System, but of course, we'd be wrong.

The Tromamercial was an actual spoof of the late-night infomercial format and even featured real celebrity testimonials from the likes of actor Andrew Stevens, comic book legend Stan Lee, *Rocky* Director John Avildsen, producers Roger Corman and Samuel Z. Arkoff (of the burning lapel story in chapter 27), and a number of other notable personalities. We shot segments with a live-studio audience and actually sold a package of goods that included a VHS tape of Troma trailers, a signed Troma movie poster, an "I Love Toxie" sticker and an audio cassette of Troma movie-theme songs.

I worked closely with Lloyd and Michael to write and produce the Tromamercial, and when it came time to start shooting the segments for it, Lloyd suggested that I should direct it. While I had been very active on Troma sets as a writer and producer, I had never actually directed any filmed scenes before, although I had studied stage directing in college. But who was I to look a gift horse in the mouth? I said "sure, I'd love to..." and the next thing I knew I was planning shots, instructing actors, and calling out the proverbial "action." I didn't really know what I was doing, but I had watched Lloyd in action enough to be able to fake it until I made it, and while definitely goofy, the tongue-in-cheek, inside spoof of both Troma and infomercials achieved the desired effect. It is fun and funny.

The lesson, of course, is to seize opportunities when they present themselves, and, as important, don't let self-doubt stand in the way of self-improvement and gaining new experience. Every expert in every field, no matter how accomplished, started with the first time. Every single director in Hollywood at one point had never directed before. Just because you "never did it before," that should never be the reason for not attempting something. On the contrary, if you've never done something and are given the opportunity to do it, that should be even more reason to say yes and do your best. By definition, it will only be the first time once, and after that you'll only have the opportunity to improve.

So, for the Tromamercial I shared writing, producing, and directing credit with Lloyd and Michael, and when asked if I've ever directed before I can always say yes.

I thank Lloyd and Michael, and Troma, for all the first times I was able to check off my list during my stint in Tromaville. I learned a lot, and hope some of it may have worn off on you through these pages.

Chapter 35

● ● ●

IN CONCLUSION: LESSONS LEARNED FROM TOXIE

If you are still reading and have stuck with me this far, I hope you have enjoyed my tales from Tromaville and found them both entertaining and on some odd level, inspiring. I would not have written this book if I did not actually believe that there were lessons to be learned from the wacky world I lived in for seven years as a resident of Tromaville. After all, I've held onto these stories for over two decades, and I really have applied these very lessons to my own winding, but generally successful, career as an entrepreneur and marketer. If just one of these lessons has sparked something within you and made you think differently about your next move, then I know I have succeeded and my seven years of exposure to Toxic wast…er, well, exposure to Toxie, was not for naught.

With that in mind, and to increase my odds of succeeding in inspiring you, let's take a few moments and pages to review everything I know about business and marketing that I learned from *The Toxic Avenger*:

CHAPTER 2: THE TROMA BUILDING

While it may have bordered on dingy, and was hardly a prestige address, Troma owned The Troma Building in the heart of Hell's Kitchen, which proved to be a real cost savings as well as a real valuable asset in the end.

Real estate can be a smart business investment. Owning your office versus renting it can save the day, especially if revenue-generating tenants can occupy a portion of the space.

CHAPTER 4: TRAILER TRASH

When asked about the trailer he just showed me, I was not afraid to give an honest answer, even if it wasn't entirely positive. Lloyd didn't know me from the proverbial hole in the wall, yet he was open to asking me my opinion and more importantly, he listened to what I said, and was willing to react to a good idea, regardless of its source.

It is good to share your ideas. Don't be afraid to give someone a good idea or help them without expecting anything in return. Holding back your ideas because you think they are precious or valuable or because you are afraid someone will steal them is just a way to hold yourself back.

And as Lloyd showed, be open to change and to new ideas, regardless of where they come from. Sometimes you have to let go of "ownership" and acknowledge ways to improve or accept a better idea, even if it means pulling back from your idea. I had no track record to speak of, and yet when Lloyd heard a good idea, a better choice, he was ready and willing to discard what he had already done and make a change that he perceived to be for the better. And it cost money to change the trailer and the posters and flyers. But it was the right move.

How can you be more open to accepting suggestions and new ideas?

CHAPTER 7: BRANDING BEGINS ON THE GROUND FLOOR

Troma was and is one of the few movie studios that indeed created a successful brand, where, like for Disney, fans would want to see a movie just because it was a Troma movie. Fans know what to expect and know that the brand will deliver something that is highly likely to meet that expectation.

That's what branding is all about—establishing trusted consumer expectations. It doesn't matter if the expectations are for family-friendly fare or tasteless, sophomoric gore, as long as the brand message is well established and consistent, it works.

And, a strong brand must be rooted in something accessible—something consumers can relate to either by association or aspiration. Something that makes them feel that by supporting the brand, they are part of a community or tribe of like-minded consumers and fans. This is as true for toothpaste as it is for a cookie or, in this book's case, a low-budget independent movie studio.

CHAPTER 8: THE POWER OF WE

At Troma, it was practically beat into my young, impressionable mind that "I" was a bad word (or, at least, a bad letter.) There was no "I," only "we." To this day, I prefer to say "we" in business correspondence and it took me a long time after my tenure in Tromaville to not feel a touch of guilt when I wrote "I" in a business letter or e-mail.

In truth, all these years later, I have come to believe that "we" truly is more often much better and more accurate. Just like making a movie, business is a very collaborative process. Unless you are truly a sole proprietor it is unlikely that there are many, if any, business projects or accomplishments that are truly achieved by you alone. If you are an employee or an employer, you are part of a team, and for most things you might take credit for, just saying "I" is a bit disingenuous. And even if you had the lead or did most of the work yourself, saying "we" lets you share the love, and sets a great leadership example.

Even today, I often find myself cringing in meetings when I hear some-one spouting "I did this" and "I did that" when I know, as does everyone else in the room know, that the person shining the light on themselves had lots of help from other members of the organization. Try it yourself. Take note of the chronic "I" people in your midst. How do they make you feel? Try to consciously say "we" instead of "I" and see how that makes you feel? Better, right? We knew it!

CHAPTER 9: OLD YELLER (AND BE YOUR BRAND)

Consistency. It is all about consistency.

Lloyd and Michael, in the early days, were consistent yellers. Eventually, that was OK because in their consistency I found a way to accept and deal with their "loud" side. Consistency.

An effective brand must always stand for the same thing. An effective brand must be consistent. What your brand is consistent about perhaps matters far less than the fact that you are consistent in presenting the brand values. Know your brand. Decide what it stands for, good or bad, and get behind it consistently. The more consistent your brand message is, the more lasting it will be. Look at the great brands. If you ask ten people what those brands stand for, you will get ten very similar answers. They all have the same expectations of the brand.

CHAPTER 10: FIND SOMETHING TO BELIEVE IN

The common thread you will hear people say is usually that you should "pursue your passion" and find a job you are passionate about. The truth is, in my humble opinion, often the opposite. Most people do not find a job or career that exactly matches their deep inner passion. But that doesn't mean that being passionate about what you do is not important. It is. But you may need to work a bit to find that passion.

There are going to be times in your career where you are doing something that is not so great, or that you are not particularly fond of. You still need to do it well, and to do it well you need to embrace it. You need to find something about it that you can love. Find some element of the work that you can be honestly and deeply passionate about. There is always something.

It's like any good relationship. Eventually, you come to love the whole package, even if, in the beginning, it was just certain bits of him or her that you were attracted to.

Find something to believe in. It is the only way to succeed.

CHAPTER 11: SHOW UP

When making a movie, you are operating on a carefully planned, day-to-day schedule. This forces a discipline that could well serve any business. Every day of production we had to focus on the basics and make sure that, no matter what, we had the bare minimum to get through the day and stay on schedule.

Understanding the necessity of the basics was a good lesson. In business, it is very easy to get caught up in the detritus, in the details of the moment, and lose sight of the simple things that are actually far more important. You may end your day feeling that you have been productive, but have you contributed to moving forward the big picture? Have you paid attention to the basics that will lead you and your company to success, or are you just checking off tasks on a to-do list to nowhere?

CHAPTER 12: SINK OR SWIM

Your sneakers say it all. Just do it. Better to be finished than to be perfect. Better to have lost in love than never to have loved at all. There is no try, just do. Yabba dabba do.

That's the lesson. The best way to learn is simply to do. Take a chance by doing something you've never done before. Give a chance by delegating to someone who has never done it before. Of course, you need to supervise them and make sure the whole project doesn't implode, but within reason, delegate and let them make the noncritical mistakes they can learn from.

CHAPTER 13: EMBRACE YOUR VISION AND CULTURE

Culture shock: a great company culture has nothing to do with pizza and beer on Fridays, a foosball table in the lounge or a kitchen cabinet full of gourmet snacks. Those are perks, but they are not the things that actually percolate productivity and promise in an organization.

A great company culture enables and encourages employees to embody and reflect the essence of the brand in their ethic, attitude, and execution of their work. It goes deeper than office environment and is more significant than a list of core values on a whiteboard. A great company culture is one where everyone organically lives and breathes the same brand. A great culture is one where all employees understand and appreciate the DNA of the brand. They don't have to be it, but they have to believe it. At its best, culture is something that grows and thrives organically and not because someone wrote it down in a manual.

CHAPTER 14: STRATEGIC PARTNERS: BURN HOUSES, NOT BRIDGES

"If you don't ask, you don't get." I may have first heard this line from my boss at Satori, Ernie Sauer, but as a concept and process, it was hammered home to me in Tromaville. In the realm of independent (read "low- or no-budget") filmmaking, "If you don't ask, you don't get" is a worthy mantra for the production. Especially when it comes to scouting for shooting locations. With no budget, we had to play the "Glass Menagerie" card—we had to rely on the kindness of strangers. If you are direct, honest, and upfront, you'd be surprised how much you can get just by asking. And what do you have to lose? If you don't at least ask, you'll never know what the answer would have been.

CHAPTER 15: IF YOU DON'T WANT TO SWALLOW A FROG, START WITH A STUNT

As Mark Twain suggests, swallow a frog first thing in the morning. Do some really super hard shit right at the beginning to get everyone focused (and maybe a little nervous), but in truth, there's no better way to quickly bond a group of disparate people than to have them accomplish a really hard, potentially dangerous, task together. Focus is required. Teamwork is required. It is going from zero to sixty in the first few hours of working together. It forces the cream to rise to the top and quickly exposes the weak links in the chain (there were always fewer people on the crew on day two than there were on day one). It is risky, but it is also rewarding. And when it works (actually more often than not), it sets the tone for the rest of the production, with everyone diving in with a level of confidence and camaraderie that otherwise might have taken weeks to develop.

At Troma, our "frog" was usually kicking things off with a big action scene or stunt. What are the frogs you can start each day with in your business?

CHAPTER 16: REPURPOSE, ON PURPOSE

There's an action scene of a car flipping over that has appeared in multiple Troma movies. We're not talking about reshooting the same stunt. That might be considered legit. We're talking about using the same actual footage, again and again, film after film. This bit of cinematic trickery was actually good marketing!

While the impetus of the Troma Team might have initially been to cut corners and save money and screen time by using the same stunt footage in film after film, once again the studio from Hell('s Kitchen) demonstrated an uncanny understanding of content marketing long before the term content marketing became a leading business buzzword. Today content is beyond king; it is Almighty as companies and brands struggle to create content to feed their famished social platforms and native advertisements. The kind of repurposing of content that came instinctively to Troma, today is a strategy. Repurposing marketing content is "de rigueur" for videos, pictures, and blog posts are shared and reused across platforms and medium. Every bit of branded content is its own "car flip" ready to flip from Instagram to Facebook to Snapchat to Twitter and back again.

CHAPTER 17: ALWAYS SALUTE THE SCHWAG

Like trusty Boy and Girl Scouts, always carrying schwag meant you are always prepared. You never know when you will have the opportunity to leave behind that sales flyer or other pieces of promotional schwag. At Troma, we always had something we could give away in our pockets, bags, or cars. Never go anywhere empty handed. And don't forget the power of a good T-shirt. We would print bright-red (and sometimes yellow) "I made the Troma Team" T-shirts by the hundreds. They were inexpensive thin cotton tees with a big Troma logo on them, and people loved them. When it came to production time, our "I-made-the-Troma-Team" tees were like a liquid currency. They were our beads, our wampum, our bitcoin, and often our savior. It is amazing what regular, unassuming humans will do or give up in exchange for a free T-shirt.

Have you printed your shirts yet? What are you waiting for?

CHAPTER 18: PLAYING BY THE RULES

While in some cases rules can be restrictive, when they are simple, direct and core to your objective, a few good rules can help bind your team together and help keep things moving forward in a positive way. If it can work for Troma, it can work for you.

What are your business's "rules"?

CHAPTER 19: FIX IT, OR FORGET IT...FAST

This is a lesson that is easy to forget in the nonmovie world because in most businesses there is a lot more flexibility on a day-to-day basis than there is on a movie set. You may be under pressure to meet a monthly or quarterly goal, but what about losing sunlight before all the necessary pages are shot in a location you absolutely, positively can never return to after the end of the day? Movies function day to day, and that fosters a discipline that would be beneficial to apply to any business. Every day on set must contribute to the end-goal of a finished film. Is every day at your office contributing to your end-goal?

CHAPTER 20: THIS MEANS *WAR*

When it came to being in production, the lessons I learned in preparation, scheduling, and negotiation were lessons that have proven to be valuable in every career move I've made since. The discipline and planning of preproduction are something that every product launch could benefit from. Few businesses understand their processes as well as a film production, where literally every page of the script (think product roadmap) is broken down into manageable (well, hopefully manageable) chunks, to be executed according to a strict schedule, literally laid out on a schedule board for all to see. Imagine how much more efficient your business would be if it were broken down with the detail and depth even a lowly Troma production had. Every day was fully accounted for, with a breakdown of every needed element—location, actors, costumes, set pieces, props, equipment, crew, a plan to get us all there, a plan to shoot something else should Mother Nature or other forces interfere.

Of course, things were fluid and could and would change along the way, but at the onset, we had a plan that, in theory, would successfully get us from point A to point B. From having nothing to having all the necessary footage in the can to piece together the film we intended to make.

Do you have a script breakdown for your business?

CHAPTER 21: DELEGATE OR DIE

A good filmmaker, like a good businessperson, knows to "inspect what they expect" and monitor and check up on the tasks they have assigned to others.

On a movie set, it is not uncommon to have a short meeting with department heads late at night, to review the schedule for the next day and ensure, while there is still time to make adjustments, that everything delegated has been taken care of and is ready to go for the morning and day ahead.

This kind of department-head huddle is a good practice for any business. Of course, it doesn't need to be done at night, but it should be done. Check in and check up, to avoid having to check out!

CHAPTER 22: LOCATION, LOCATION, LOCATION

Scouting for and securing filming locations was by far one of my favorite aspects of making movies, and the skills and experiences handling such negotiations are some of the most valuable I've carried forward throughout my career. Relationships, sincerity, authenticity, and directness were the keys to successfully securing locations like Croton-on-Hudson, Camp Smith and Caumsett State Park. We were upfront about our needs and the content we were creating, and we were upfront about our respect for the process and responsibility to care for the people and property under our watch (remember the "Rules of Production").

CHAPTER 23: EVERYONE IS EXPENDABLE

Everyone is expendable.
　　Even me and you.
　　Don't worry about it, but don't forget it either.

CHAPTER 24: BE OPEN TO THE UNEXPECTED

Inspiration comes in many forms and often in unexpected shapes and sizes. You need to be ready to see it and embrace it (even if doing so makes you appear to be a nerdy idiot).

CHAPTER 25: INFLUENCE THE INFLUENCERS

Be real. Be authentic. Take your business seriously, but don't take yourself too seriously. Be self-aware about your business, and its role in your industry and the world. Some folks are out there saving lives and curing cancer. Most of us are not, so be true to the actual value of your products and services. That's not to diminish them, but rather to present them in the right light and context.

CHAPTER 26: YES, WE CANNES

Do you go to industry events and trade shows? In most cases, it is very hard to see direct results from attending a trade show or conference that covers the cost of being at the event. On the other hand, if you return to a show, year after year, there is a residual value to being there that doesn't go unnoticed by your customers. If you can be patient, that residual value can pay off years later, and big enough to make all the earlier "dry" years worthwhile. Yes, you Cannes!

CHAPTER 28: SLEEPING ON THE JOB

The truth is, when you're a start-up and operating on limited resources you must get creative and be willing to do things "the big guys" might not consider. For me, aside from adding a bit of intrigue and adventure to my trip, sleeping surreptitiously behind an exhibit in our conference suite (against the conference rules) saved the company money and me time. I was happy to be taking one for the Troma Team.

Would you make a similar sacrifice for your team? Have you ever put up with unusual conditions just to get the job done?

CHAPTER 29: RAISING YOUR HAND

When new opportunities arise for your business, before you hire the so-called experts, could you create an expert from within?

CHAPTER 30: IN WHAT UNIVERSE COULD *THE TOXIC AVENGER* AND *READING RAINBOW* COEXIST?

There were many great lessons in the Troma licensing experience, and I still relish in the fact we were able to convince an award-winning PBS children's show to come under the same roof as *The Toxic Avenger*. I credit that victory to passion and creativity, and the Troma culture of authenticity. We turned the potential liability of Toxie into an asset that demonstrated the depth of our abilities. We were passionate about Toxie and could bring that passion to our approach to their show, and we had an outlook that was different, and that showed in our ideas of creative ways to make licensing work for a property that, while acclaimed and successful, didn't necessarily fit the traditional model for licensing success.

Don't be afraid to pursue an opportunity because it seems impossible (as Troma and PBS working together most certainly looked at first). In business, passion and creativity can and do overcome what might seem to be the more logical path. If you believe in it, go for it. What was our risk? The cost of some artwork mock-ups and a trip to Washington DC (and perhaps the potential embarrassment of a decided "no"). Certainly worth it.

CHAPTER 31: GIVE CREDITS WHERE CREDIT IS DUE

Don't underestimate the value of recognition. What does it cost you to acknowledge a job well done? Nothing. Yet to the person on the receiving end of that recognition it may mean a great deal. And you don't have to be the boss to offer credit. One of the most powerful ways to gain respect and admiration is to be the one who recognizes their peers and acknowledges their accomplishments both privately to them, and when appropriate, publicly. In Tromaville, where I was surrounded by folks desperately trying to find their way and do the right thing without much experience or guidance, I learned the power of giving credit and praise when someone did well.

This is not just a fact of Tromaville, though that's where the lesson hit home for me, and I've tried to be generous and aware of giving praise and recognition ever since. The truth is that numerous studies have shown that when it comes to employee motivation, recognition is often a better impetus than more money. Are you giving credit where credit is due? How can you better leverage giving recognition. And by the way, this is not just a good business practice. Giving recognition works with children if you are a parent, and with your partner, if you are in a relationship. Don't you like receiving praise? Of course, you do. So does everyone else in your world; so be the giver as often as you can. It may not have the permanence of a film credit, but the credit you give will have an impact and a positive one.

CHAPTER 32: THE STALKING DEAD

I learned a lot from Peri and the *Redneck Zombies* story. Persistence and patience are often the key to the payoff. And you must believe in yourself before anyone else will believe in you. Peri and Ed were believers. They made *Redneck Zombies* with a clear mission in mind. It *would* become a Troma Team release. They never stopped believing that, and they were more than happy to do whatever it took, even sleeping on the cold hard reality of a Hell's Kitchen stoop, just to demonstrate their unwavering belief in said mission. Granted, things don't always work out the way you want just because you believe, but your chances are certainly better if you are truly committed to your cause.

There's also a lesson in Lloyd's willingness to see talent and good in something regardless of the wrapper it shows up in. At the time we acquired *Redneck Zombies,* there was literally no such thing as a film shot only on video getting mainstream distribution. Peri and Ed's little film was the first. Lloyd knew it was good and deserved to be seen (especially by Troma fans), so he was willing to give it a shot when others would have said no solely on the fact it was not shot on film. But good is good, and Troma knows its audience. *Redneck Zombies* has enjoyed continued success as a Troma Classic ever since, and today nobody thinks twice about a "film" shot entirely on video. It is OK to be the first. Just because something has not been done before doesn't mean it can't break through and be successful. If Lloyd and Troma stuck to the conventional wisdom of the time, we'd never have touched a "film" that was not shot on film, and *Redneck Zombies* would never have found its place in film gore history.

CHAPTER 33: TACKLING NONTOXIC TECHNOLOGY

Technology is your friend. Don't be afraid to experiment with and adopt new technologies and platforms as they can readily lead to new business models and new distribution channels and audiences for your product or service. In truth, there are few better examples of technology opening new doors than the film-distribution business, and especially for a studio like Troma, which was building an extensive library of content. When I first joined Troma, the primary outlet for its movies was in theaters. Then home video came along, and films that hadn't earned a dime in years suddenly had a new life (and value) breathed into them thanks to the VHS industry. Then doors opened on cable and pay TV, and we found ourselves licensing those same movies to USA Network and other TV outlets. Then VHS became DVD, and DVD became streaming, at each juncture creating new opportunities to repurpose content (i.e., films) that were initially created for an entirely different medium.

Yes, technology often leads to disruption, but if you can figure out how to ride the wave of disruption, technology can expand, rather than constrict your business. What new tech trends can you leverage to grow your business? Can VR and AR have an impact on what you do? Mobile? Wearables? Where can you overlay your product or service on the latest new tech? If you can figure that out, you may see new ways to grow your business, just as Troma has evolved alongside tech to grow theirs.

CHAPTER 34: THE DIRECTOR'S CHAIR AND THE TROMAMERCIAL

The lesson, of course, is to seize opportunities when they present themselves, and, as important, don't let self-doubt stand in the way of self-improvement and gaining new experience. Every expert in every field, no matter how accomplished, started with the first time. Every single director in Hollywood at one point had never directed before. Just because you "never did it before," that should never be the reason for not attempting something. On the contrary, if you've never done something and are given the opportunity to do it, that should be even more reason to say yes and do your best. By definition, it will only be the first time once, and after that you'll only have the opportunity to improve.

Chapter 36

●　●　●

CUT!

And so you have it. I've shared the lights, camera, and some of the action I experienced as a young, impressionable lad in the land of Troma. While the title of this book credits Toxie for all I learned, I'd be remiss if I didn't acknowledge Lloyd and Michael for creating an equal-opportunity Tromaville, where anyone who truly wanted to learn and gain experience actually could. Sure, it was often a shit show, but isn't that life? Nothing is as easy as you would think, and rewards are hidden in the most unexpected places.

A career, especially in this technologically advanced day and age, is most often a long and winding road (sure, that's a discreet Beatles reference), and the best way to have a long and successful career is to relish in the journey and always be open to be learning from every twist and turn. Those lessons, if you let them, will prove to be of value no matter where your path may take you.

And of course, you never know who will prove to be a valuable mentor. It could even be a hideously deformed creature of superhuman size and strength!

Thanks, Toxie!

Jeff Sass
Fort Lauderdale, Florida
January 2017

EPILOGUE

In case you were wondering...

I decided to write this book inspired by a five-minute presentation I gave in 2012. As a "dad blogger," I had been invited to attend a Ford event in Detroit, Michigan, which included a press event at the International Auto Show. As part of the Ford event, I signed up to give an "Ignite" presentation at one of the evening festivities.

The Ignite format is a fun one. Basically, you have to give a five-minute presentation that teaches or inspires (that ignites some thinking). You have to give your presentation with exactly twenty slides, which display for exactly fifteen seconds each. The challenge is that the slides are set to play automatically. As the presenter, you have no control over them. You start your presentation and *boom*, every fifteen seconds the slide changes, and at exactly the five-minute mark, your presentation is over.

It was for this short Ignite presentation that I had the idea to connect my experiences working at Troma with real business and marketing lessons, and I called the presentation "Everything I Know about Business, I Learned from *The Toxic Avenger*."

Toward the end of the five-minute presentation, I said, "I could go on and on...I could write a book about this, and I probably will..."

So, it took me five years to turn those five minutes into the book you have just read. I hope it was worth the wait.

You can watch that five-minute presentation here: www.toxie. marketing.

ABOUT THE AUTHOR

While early in his career, Jeff Sass was making B-movies, he has spent more recent years in the C-suite as a COO, CEO, and CMO. With a career spanning the entertainment, computer-game, mobile, and Internet worlds, he has written and produced for film and TV, and he has been a tech start-up entrepreneur. A frequent speaker on entrepreneurship, mobile marketing, domain names, and social media, Jeff Sass has had articles appear in *Forbes*, *Entrepreneur*, *AdAge*, and many other publications. As the father of three, he has also been a prolific "dad blogger," participating in influencer campaigns for brands including Intel, Sony, Ford, LG, Asus, and others. Despite this seemingly successful career, Jeff Sass is happy to admit that everything he knows about business and marketing, he learned from *The Toxic Avenger*.

For a more detailed Touch of Sass, please visit www.JeffreySass.com.

The author in a cameo appearance (Screen capture
from *The Toxic AVENGER Part II*)

The author as "the Doctor" (Screen Capture from *Sgt. Kabukiman NYPD*)

Made in the USA
Middletown, DE
04 March 2020